PETRA ZIMMERMANN

Schmuck
Jewellery

ARNOLDSCHE

Inhalt | Contents

Eye-Catchers and Thought-Provokers

Petra Zimmermann's jewellery is refulgent with a sensuous interpretation of glamour. It glitters and sparkles, confronting the viewer with intense, vibrant colours. Don't let yourself be bedazzled by this opulent façade, however – otherwise you may miss the many-layered play of references and ambivalent legibility behind it, and therein lies the true quality of her jewellery. Petra Zimmermann manages to create objects that are not merely "beautiful", and whose raison d'être is not exhausted by their decorative function. On second glance, they reveal themselves as "thought-provokers", posing aesthetic questions about the appeal, value and expiry date of beauty. Petra Zimmermann tackles these questions with a conceptual strategy that first revealed itself in an early series of rings and bracelets, and which continues to constitute the foundation of her work.

At the time when this seminal first series was created, Petra Zimmermann was studying sculpture at the University of Applied Arts in Vienna. One of the features of her characteristic approach is to take found materials – in particular costume jewellery from the first half of the 20th century – and to cast them in a medium, usually coloured plastic. This gives the found jewellery objects the same prominent status in her works that is normally assigned to precious gemstones in traditional jewellery. The plastic form of the ring serves, in a sense, as a pedestal for the presentation of the found object. Zimmermann herself described these works unemotionally and concisely as "Jewellery in Jewellery" – this was the title of the exhibition staged at the Biró gallery in Munich in the year 2000, at which a larger group of these pieces was presented for the first time. Over and above the reference to the formal strategy used, the title of the series also points to a self-referential reflection about jewellery, in jewellery. Making use of the strict conceptual confines of her „Schmuck im Schmuck" ("Jewellery in Jewellery") strategy, Zimmermann investigates not only the formal variants revealed by contrasting found materials with her own individual designs, but also the resulting shifts in levels of meaning. Particularly in the earlier rings, the integration of formal elements from her "found footage" results in varied and astoundingly complex works. A ring set with stones produced in 1998 is an example of a comparatively simple design by Petra Zimmermann: Half of the ring is cast in a flat, almost rectangular block of plastic. The translucency of the plastic allows the ring to remain visible, and it is "doubled" by virtue of the way that the metal ring is embedded in the plastic. This "meta ring" within the plastic expresses the concept of "Jewellery in Jewellery" in its purest form. In turn, this is further emphasised by the visibility of the formal means used in the execution of the work, as premised by modern design principles. With her almost "ready-made" approach to the presentation of the found ring, one gets the impression that Zimmermann wishes to challenge the wearer/observer to reflect on the qualities and potential of jewellery.

A later ring produced in 2001 started with a triangular costume brooch set with blue rhinestones, overlaid with a slightly offset V of white rhinestones. Here, the basic form of the piece of jewellery is drawn into the third dimension by ensconcing it in a pyramid-shaped ring, which is also coloured blue. In contrast to the previous example, the plastic form in this work plays a more important, interpretive role with regard to the brooch it

Eyecatcher und Denkstücke

Wolfram Otto

Petra Zimmermanns Schmuck ist ganz einer lustvollen Interpretation von Glamour verschrieben. Glitzernd, funkelnd und farbintensiv präsentiert er sich dem Betrachter. Doch sollte man sich nicht nur blenden lassen und einen Blick hinter die opulente Oberfläche wagen, um das vielschichtige Spiel mit Zitaten und ambivalenter Lesbarkeit nicht zu verpassen, denn darin liegt die Qualität ihres Schmucks. Es gelingt Petra Zimmermann, Objekte zu schaffen, die nicht einfach nur "schön" sind und sich in ihrer schmückenden Funktion erschöpfen. Auf den zweiten Blick entfalten sie sich vielmehr zu "Denkstücken" über die ästhetischen Fragen nach dem Reiz, Wert und Ablaufdatum von Schönheit. Diese Fragen verhandelt Petra Zimmermann mit Hilfe einer konzeptuellen Strategie, die zum ersten Mal in einer frühen Serie von Ringen und Armreifen deutlich wurde und bis heute die Grundlage ihrer Arbeit bildet.

Als diese richtungsweisende Serie entstand, studierte Petra Zimmermann Bildhauerei an der Universität für angewandte Kunst in Wien. Zu ihrer charakteristischen Vorgehensweise gehört es, vorgefundenes Material – bevorzugt Modeschmuck aus der ersten Hälfte des 20. Jahrhunderts – in Trägerformen aus meist eingefärbtem Kunststoff einzugießen. Den gefundenen Schmuckobjekten kommt dabei eben jener herausgehobene Platz zu, der bei klassischem Juwelenschmuck wertvollen Edelsteinen vorbehalten ist. Die Kunststoffringform dient dem gefundenen Objekt gewissermaßen als „Sockel".
Zimmermann selbst subsummierte diese Arbeiten lapidar unter der Überschrift „Schmuck im Schmuck" – so lautete auch der Titel der Ausstellung in der Münchner Galerie Biró im Jahr 2000, in deren Rahmen erstmals eine größere Gruppe dieser Schmuckstücke zu sehen war. Der Titel der Serie verweist über eine reine Beschreibung der formalen Strategie hinaus auf eine selbstreferentielle Reflexion von Schmuck über Schmuck. Die konzeptuelle Strenge von „Schmuck im Schmuck" diente Zimmermann dazu, nicht nur formale Varianten in der Gegenüberstellung von Vorgefundenem und individueller Formgebung auszuloten, sondern auch die sich daraus ergebenden Verschiebungen der Bedeutungsebenen zu erkunden. Vor allem bei den frühen Ringen entstehen durch das Aufgreifen formaler Elemente des „found footage" variantenreiche und verblüffend komplexe Arbeiten. Eine für Petra Zimmermann vergleichsweise reduzierte Formgebung zeigt ein mit Steinen besetzter Ring von 1998: Er ist bis zur Hälfte in eine flache, annähernd rechteckige Kunststoffform eingegossen. Der Ring bleibt durch die Transluzenz des Kunststoffs sichtbar und erfährt eine Doppelung durch die in den Kunststoff eingearbeitete metallische Ringform. Bei diesem "Meta-Ring" tritt die Idee von „Schmuck im Schmuck" in ihrer reinsten Form zu Tage. Unterstützt wird sie dabei durch die dem modernen Gestaltungscredo der Offenlegung formaler Mittel geschuldete Ausführung des Ringes. Zimmermann scheint durch ihre Methode der beinahe Ready-made-artigen Präsentation des vorgefundenen Ringes ein Angebot an den Träger/Betrachter machen zu wollen, sich über die Qualitäten und Potentiale von Schmuck Gedanken zu machen.
Ausgangsmaterial eines späteren Ringes von 2001 ist eine dreieckige Modeschmuckbrosche aus gefassten blauen Strasssteinen, die von einer leicht versetzt angebrachten

Ring | Ring, 1998

contains. Use of the almost trivially historical connotations of the pyramid shape make it clear that these ring shapes are not intended merely as presentation pedestals: they are part of the project, of the juxtaposition and contrasting of references.

The "Jewellery in Jewellery" works are the result of a quest for a contemporary aesthetic statement in the charged area of intersection between author jewellery and fine art. Petra Zimmermann finally decided to study art after participating in a course taught by Peter Skubic at the Summer Academy in Salzburg, where she first became acquainted with the foundations of author jewellery, and also a brief interlude studying jewellery with Karol Weisslechner at the Academy in Bratislava. She now says that the open dialogue she experienced in Vienna gave her a new perspective on both the problems and the potential of jewellery as an artistic medium. This dialogue was strongly influenced by the neo-conceptual movements of the 1990s, for which Vienna was one of the main focal points. In this context, it is possible to see a certain analogous relationship to the self-referential approach of context art in Zimmermann's self-reflective jewellery work. Drawing on the conceptual movements in the 1960s and 70s, context art focused on analysis of the conditions in which fine art was produced. The return to this approach by a generation of young artists was motivated by their unease at the neo-expressive tendencies of the 1980s, the increasing commercialisation of the art market and the resulting questions regarding the critical potential of fine art.

In the 1960s and 70s, the process of redefining and broadening the fundamental terminology of art was important and necessary for the establishment of author jewellery as an art form. In the aftermath of this development, however, Petra Zimmermann found herself searching for an approach that would legitimise her own artistic work in the jewellery medium: Her solution was to adopt the self-referential strategy of context art in her work by making her central focus the concept of jewellery itself and jewellery as a cultural phenomenon.

Strikingly, it is precisely this external perspective that enables her to pursue her own fascination with the conventional aspects of jewellery – her enjoyment of the play with seductive surfaces and glamorous presentation and decoration of the individual. Her investigation of the surfaces of everyday culture cannot be dismissed as a mere personal infatuation, however. In the 1990s the "aestheticisation" of everyday life grew to such an extent that it became a dominant social phenomenon, one that the art world could not ignore. The ironic nature "glamour" as imposed by the fashion industry became the epitome of the cult of superficial values. On the one hand, this cult gave artists reason for criticism, some of it biting – for example in Bret Easton Ellis' novel Glamorama ("We'll slide down the surface of things") and the collage-like overlays of everyday aesthetic fragments in the work of Michel Majerus. At the same time, there were also movements that focused on the more positive aspects of the aestheticisation of everyday culture in areas like fashion, design and club culture. These can be represented by the approaches taken by artists like Wolfgang Tillmans, Tobias Rehberger and Jorge Pardo.

Zimmermann's "Jewellery in Jewellery" series clearly reflects a critical view of jewellery as a cultural phenomenon, and the fashion jewellery components can be seen as the epitome of false appearances, superficiality and hedonism. At the same time, she makes no bones about her own personal enthusiasm for the pieces' own beauty. In this she goes beyond emotionless conceptual analysis, implementing her "Jewellery in Jewellery" concept to cast an historical and sentimental gaze on the glamorous aspects of jewellery.

Ring | Ring, 2001

V-Form aus weißem Strass überlagert wird. Die Grundform der Bijouterie wird in die dritte Dimension gezogen, sie wird zu einer pyramidalen, wiederum blau eingefärbten Ringform. Im Vergleich zum vorigen Stück kommt der Kunststoffform hier in Bezug auf das eingegossene Schmuckstück eine gewichtigere interpretatorische Rolle zu. Durch den Rückgriff auf die beinahe trivial-historisch konnotierte Pyramidenform wird deutlich, dass diese Ringformen nicht nur als Sockel fungieren: Sie sind Teil eines Projekts der Gegenüberstellung von Zitaten.

Die „Schmuck im Schmuck"-Arbeiten stellen das Resultat der Suche nach einer zeitgemäßen ästhetischen Aussage im Spannungsbereich zwischen Autorenschmuck und Bildender Kunst dar. Nachdem Petra Zimmermann durch die Teilnahme an einem von Peter Skubic geleiteten Kurs im Rahmen der Sommerakademie Salzburg mit den Ansätzen des Autorenschmucks in Kontakt gekommen war, entschied sie sich, nach einer kurzen Episode des Schmuck-Studiums an der Akademie in Bratislava bei Karol Weisslechner, letztlich für das Kunststudium. Die Offenheit des dort stattfindenden Diskurses ermöglichte ihr nach eigenen Aussagen einen neuen Blick auf Problemstellungen, aber auch auf Potentiale der Idee, Schmuck als künstlerisches Medium zu verstehen. Geprägt war dieser Diskurs von den neokonzeptuellen Strömungen der 1990er Jahre, die in Wien eines ihrer Zentren hatten. So lässt sich in Zimmermanns selbstreflexiver Auseinandersetzung mit Schmuck eine gewisse Analogie zum selbstreferentiellen Ansatz der Kontextkunst erkennen. Diese hatte in Anlehnung an die konzeptuellen Strömungen der 1960er und 70er Jahre ihren Fokus auf die Analyse der Rahmenbedingungen von Bildender Kunst gerichtet. Motiviert war der Rückgriff der jüngeren Künstlergeneration auf diesen Ansatz durch das Unbehagen gegenüber den neoexpressiven Tendenzen der 1980er Jahre, der zunehmenden Kommerzialisierung des Kunstmarktes und der daraus resultierenden Frage nach den kritischen Potentialen Bildender Kunst.

Waren in den 1960er und 70er Jahren Neudefinitionen und Begriffserweiterungen wichtig und notwendig, um den Autorenschmuck überhaupt erst als Kunstform zu etablieren, so suchte Petra Zimmermann nun nach einem Ansatz, der für sie eine künstlerische Auseinandersetzung im Medium Schmuck erst legitimierte: Sie übernimmt die selbstreferentielle Strategie der Kontextkunst in ihr Schmuckschaffen, indem sie den Schmuckbegriff und Schmuck als kulturelles Phänomen ins Zentrum ihrer Arbeit stellt. Bemerkenswerterweise ist es gerade diese Außenperspektive, die es ihr ermöglicht, ihrer Faszination für die konventionelleren Aspekte von Schmuck – der Lust am Spiel mit verführerischen Oberflächen und der glamourösen Inszenierung der Person – nachzugehen. Diese Auseinandersetzung mit den Oberflächen der Alltagskultur kann aber keineswegs als rein persönliche Vorliebe abgetan werden. In den 1990er Jahren uferte die Ästhetisierung der Alltagswelt zu einem die Gesellschaft vereinnahmenden Phänomen aus, dem sich auch die Kunstwelt nicht entziehen konnte. Zum Inbegriff des Kultes um die Oberfläche geriet die von der Modeindustrie forcierte Ironisierung von "Glamour".

So bot dieser Kult Künstlern einerseits Anlass zu bisweilen bissiger Kritik, man denke etwa an Bret Easton Ellis' Roman „Glamorama" („We'll slide down the surface of things") oder an die Collage-artigen Überlagerungen alltagsästhetischer Fragmente bei Michel Majerus. Es entstanden aber auch Ansätze, welche die positiven Aspekte der Ästhetisierung der Alltagskultur im Hinblick auf Mode, Design und Clubkultur beleuchteten. Stellvertretend seien hier die Positionen von Wolfgang Tillmans, Tobias Rehberger oder Jorge Pardo genannt.

Petra Zimmermann is continuing to use historic costume jewellery brooches in the further development of her rings and bracelets, but we can now observe a change in her design vocabulary. Increasingly, reduced geometrical forms are being replaced by amorphous, organic designs. For example, in a ring made in 2009, the plastic form of the ring no longer constitutes the "avant-garde" counterpart to the charming playfulness of the brooch; instead, the ring actually reinforces the form of the brooch with soft curves of its own. Only the neon yellow colour of the plastic interrupts this harmony, undoing the impression of an original design and pointing a reference towards the historical art sources. Zimmermann takes her selected objets trouvés and tailors individual, amorphously technoid forms to surround and enclose them. Stylistically, they are positioned somewhere between floral art nouveau, futuristic plastic and ergonomic design.

Whilst the rings Petra Zimmermann created in the 1990s transported her message more forcefully than the bracelets, the latter have been taking on an increasingly prominent role in her later works, with an ever more complex layering of quotation-like references. Zimmermann makes use of the bracelets' potential for more panorama-like arrangement of her found materials, in contrast to the rings, where the fragmentary nature of the confronted references comes to the fore. The first bracelet to make full use of this potential was produced in 2007: In this work, the entire outer surface of an ordinary bangle from H&M is veritably overrun by a scintillating layer of rhinestone brooches, as though this might be able to create a moment of overview in a world of rushing surfaces.

We find a continuation of this approach in a later bracelet, in which the overview quality is expanded in favour of more multi-layered historical references. Here too, the entire outer surface of the bracelet is made over with found fashion jewellery brooches, but here a base form fashioned from plastic is used instead of a bracelet purchased from a department store. Petra Zimmermann added obsidians to replace the missing rhinestones that had been broken out of the historical jewellery pieces in the course of time. The amorphously organic design of the bracelet surface also reflects the naturalistic motif of these volcanic glass insets. Here too, Zimmermann's use of ornamental overlays in combination with the sensual motif of the amorphous surfaces is a reference to the stylistic canon of the Vienna Secession.

Until 2003 she consciously excluded brooches from her own work, but then her decision to investigate their special role as jewellery pieces became as passionate as her earlier rejection had been. The brooch is the only piece of jewellery that is attached to the clothing rather than being worn directly on the body. Originally derived from the antique clasp, in the course of the centuries the brooch lost function as a fastener and became entirely decorative. As a purposeless object, it then advanced to become the most popular form of jewellery in modern author jewellery, because it gives artists the greatest degree of freedom in their designs.

Petra Zimmermann's first series of figurative brooches was titled "Cut-Outs and Pin-Ups", a name that describes her formal strategy and her attitude to her message in the same way as the earlier "Jewellery in Jewellery" title. The brooches' basic designs are based on silhouettes of female forms in stereotype pinup poses. In her brooches Petra Zimmermann's interest is focused on the actual presentation of bodies within a jewellery object, in contrast to her rings and bracelets, where the glamour theme is really restricted to the pieces' self-determined presentation by the wearer. The bodies are repre-

Ring | Ring, 2009

Armreif | Bracelet, 2007

Armreif | Bracelet, 2009

Zimmermanns „Schmuck im Schmuck"-Serie ist zwar geprägt von einem kritischen Blick auf das kulturelle Phänomen Schmuck, und das verwendete Bijouterie-Material kann als Inbegriff für falschen Schein, Oberflächlichkeit und Hedonismus bezeichnet werden. Zugleich macht sie aber keinen Hehl aus ihrer persönlichen Begeisterung für dessen Schönheit. Sie geht so über eine nüchterne konzeptuelle Analyse hinaus und nutzt ihre objektivierende „Schmuck im Schmuck"-Strategie, um einen historisch-sentimentalen Blick auf die glamourösen Aspekte von Schmuck zu werfen.

Während Petra Zimmermann für die Weiterentwicklung der Ringe und Armreifen weiterhin historische Modeschmuckbroschen verwendet, zeichnet sich in der Formensprache eine Veränderung ab. Zunehmend weichen reduzierte geometrische Formen einer organisch-amorphen Gestaltung. So bildet die Kunststoffform eines Ringes von 2009 nicht mehr den „avantgardistischen" Gegenpart zur lieblich anmutenden Verspieltheit der Brosche, sondern unterstützt diese mit dem weichen Schwung der Ringform. Lediglich die neongelbe Einfärbung des Kunststoffs stört diese Harmonie, bricht den Eindruck originärer Gestaltung und verweist auf den kunsthistorischen Formenfundus. Zimmermann schneidert den ausgewählten Fundstücken individuelle, technoid-amorphe, stilistisch irgendwo zwischen floralem Jugendstil, futuristischer Plastik und Ergonomie-Design angesiedelte Formen auf bzw. um den Leib.

Transportieren in den1990er Jahren die Ringe Petra Zimmermanns ihr Anliegen nachdrücklicher als die Armreifen, gewinnen gerade diese in den späteren Ausformungen an Bedeutung in der immer komplexer werdenden Übereinanderlagerung zitathafter Verweise. Steht bei ihren Ringen das Fragmentarische der konfrontierten Zitate im Vordergrund, nutzt Zimmermann bei den Armreifen das Potential der panoramaartigen Anordnung des Vorgefundenen. Erstmals schöpft ein Armreif von 2007 dieses Potential voll aus: eine schillernde Strassbroschenschicht überwuchert die gesamte Außenfläche eines gewöhnlichen H&M-Armreifs gerade so, als könne dadurch ein Moment des Überblicks in einer Welt der rasenden Oberflächen entstehen.

Dieser Ansatz findet seine Fortsetzung in einem späteren Armreif, der das Überblickartige zugunsten vielschichtigerer historischer Verweise ausdehnt. Auch hier wird die gesamte Außenfläche des Armreifs mit vorgefundenen Modeschmuckbroschen bespielt, wobei statt eines Kaufhaus-Armreifens eine aus Kunststoff angefertigte Trägerform zum Einsatz kommt. Aus den historischen Bijouterien im Laufe der Zeit herausgebrochene Strasssteine wurden durch Obsidiane ersetzt. Die amorph-organische Gestaltung der Armreif-Oberfläche greift das naturalistische Motiv des eingearbeiteten vulkanischen Gesteinsglases auf. Auch hier verweist Zimmermann durch die ornamentartigen Überlagerungen in Kombination mit dem sensualistischen Motiv der amorphen Oberfläche auf den Formenkanon der Wiener Secession.

Während Petra Zimmermann bis 2003 die Brosche aus ihrem Schaffen bewusst ausklammerte, war die Entscheidung, sich mit deren Sonderstellung als Schmuckstück auseinanderzusetzen, ebenso leidenschaftlich wie zuvor deren Ablehnung. Die Brosche ist das einzige Schmuckstück, das nicht direkt am Körper getragen, sondern an die Kleidung geheftet wird. Entstanden aus der antiken Fibel, verlor sie über die Jahrhunderte ihre die Kleidung fixierende Funktion und wurde zur reinen Applikation. So avancierte sie als zweckfreies Objekt zur beliebtesten Schmuckform im zeitgenössischen Autorenschmuck überhaupt, denn sie gewährt die größte Gestaltungsfreiheit.

sented as forms in plastic, and the other basic elements of the figures like clothing and facial features are indicated schematically with artistic colouring of the plastic material. The frozen, stereotype poses are exaggerated by the addition of rhinestones set in the piece: the female body is reduced to an object-like base, a medium for the glittering surfaces. This almost maliciously ironic interpretation is emphasised further by an often grotesque distortion of the facial features – an effect resulting from the melting of the faces' outlines. In the "Jewellery in Jewellery" series, Petra Zimmermann was only able to approach a sensuous play with surfaces by means of a self-reflexive jewellery strategy; in these early brooches, in contrast, it seems that the investigation of images of the human body was initially enabled through the media-inspired reduction of the female body to a stereotype pose.

In the brooches of the "Cut-Outs and Pin-Ups" series, the focus is an ironic criticism of the dis-individualising, object-like exhibition of bodies. In the later figurative brooches, the basic material is still images of presented femininity, most taken from fashion photography, but now with multi-layered overlays. Here too, Zimmermann continues to use plastic as the base medium for the presentation of her images; however, the found images are no longer transferred with artistic methods but are now directly cast into the plastic. In the course of this process the printing ink becomes separated from the paper, and at the end all that is left is an "imprint" of the motif in the plastic. The original image is completely preserved – backed with gold leaf and then back-painted or over-painted and accentuated with jewellery fragments.

And so the neutral, quotation-like use of the found image actually moves into the foreground vis-à-vis the more interpretive artistic incorporation utilised in the "Cut-Outs and Pin-Ups" series. In a brooch produced in 2008, the image of a model posing with a slightly open mouth is frugally decorated with black beads that look a little like cryptic speech bubbles – rather as though Zimmermann wanted to place a statement in the mouth of a model otherwise damned to silent anonymity.

In general, the models "used" by Petra Zimmermann in her works can be seen as empathetically individualised figures. This approach remains a constant in her following figurative works. However, the stereotype nature of the images means that what is created here are only possibilities. The subject is never a specific personal story. Petra Zimmermann's consistent pursuit of her strategy of contrasting visual quotations, in combination with the increasing breadth of her themes, enables her to create tableau-like assemblies. For example, a necklace produced in 2008 follows in the tradition of double portraits like Warhol's "Double Elvis" and Jeff Wall's "Double Self-Portrait". Both these works deal with the implications of the duplication of an individual through media: in the case of Warhol, the duplication of an image of a pop icon; for Wall, the duplication of himself. In her necklace, Zimmermann adds a new variant by taking images of two different models and contrasting them on an equal footing, decorated with identical, mirror-image jewellery fragments. This looks like a reference to an amulet worn around the neck that shows an image of the wearer's beloved when opened. And so the doubling of the jewellery attributes appear on the one hand to be an ironic visual allusion to something like genetic kinship, and on the other, with equally ironic undertones, a reference to the way that the model portraits can be read as different expressions of something that nonetheless has an "intrinsic" relatedness.

Der Titel „Cut-Outs and Pin-Ups" der ersten Serie figurativer Broschen beschreibt analog zu „Schmuck im Schmuck" formale Strategie und inhaltliche Ausrichtung der Arbeiten Petra Zimmermanns. Ausgangspunkt sind entlang der Körperkontur ausgeschnittene Abbildungen weiblicher Körper, die in klischeehaften „Pin-up"-Posen zu sehen sind. Während bei den Ringen und Armreifen die Thematisierung von Glamour letztlich auf die selbstbestimmte Inszenierung der Trägerin/des Trägers hinausläuft, richtet sich Petra Zimmermanns Interesse an den Broschen nun auf die Thematisierung inszenierter Körper innerhalb des Schmuckobjekts. Diese werden von ihr in Kunststoff übertragen, wobei Grundelemente der Figur wie Kleidung und Gesichtszüge durch eine malerische Einfärbung des Kunststoffs schemenhaft nachgezeichnet werden. Die klischeehaft erstarrte Pose erfährt durch zusätzlich eingearbeitete Strasssteine eine Überzeichnung: Der weibliche Körper wird auf einen objekthaften Träger glitzernder Oberflächen reduziert. Diese beinahe boshafte ironische Auffassung wird durch das oftmals fratzenhafte Entstellen der Gesichtszüge noch unterstützt – ein Effekt, der aus den zerflossenen Outlines der Gesichter resultiert. Während Petra Zimmermann in der „Schmuck im Schmuck"-Serie eine Annäherung an ein lustvolles Spiel mit Oberflächen nur mittels einer schmuckreflexiven Strategie möglich war, scheint die Auseinandersetzung mit dem Abbild des menschlichen Körpers bei diesen frühen Broschen erst durch die Thematisierung der medialen Reduktion des weiblichen Körpers auf eine klischeehafte Pose möglich.

Steht bei den Broschen der „Cut-Outs and Pin-Ups"-Serie die ironische Kritik der entindividualisierenden objekthaften Zurschaustellung von Körpern im Vordergrund, dienen bei späteren figurativen Broschen Abbildungen inszenierter Weiblichkeit, meist aus der Modefotografie, weiterhin als Ausgangsmaterial, werden aber vielschichtiger überlagert. Dabei dient Zimmermann der Kunststoff nach wie vor als Bildträger. Die vorgefundenen Abbildungen werden jedoch nicht mehr mit malerischen Mitteln übertragen, sondern direkt in den Kunststoff eingegossen. Bei diesem Vorgang löst sich die Druckfarbe vom Papier, sodass letztlich nur der „Abdruck" des Motivs im Kunststoff haften bleibt. Das Ursprungsbild bleibt vollständig erhalten – mit Blattgold hinterlegt, dann hinteroder übermalt und mit Schmuck-Fragmenten akzentuiert.

So tritt die zitathaft neutrale Verwendung der vorgefundenen Abbildung gegenüber der stärker interpretativen malerischen Einarbeitung der „Cut-Outs and Pin-Ups"-Serie in den Vordergrund. Die Abbildung eines mit leicht geöffnetem Mund posierenden Models wird in einer Brosche von 2008 spärlich mit schwarzen Perlen bestückt, die wie kryptische Text-Bubbles wirken – geradeso als wolle Petra Zimmermann dem zu anonymer Sprachlosigkeit verdammten Model eine mögliche Aussage in den Mund legen.

Brosche | Brooch, 2008

Tendenziell lassen sich die von Petra Zimmermann „benutzten" Models als empathisch individualisierte Figuren lesen. Diese Vorgehensweise bleibt eine Konstante in den folgenden figurativen Arbeiten. Wobei durch die Klischeehaftigkeit der Abbilder immer nur Möglichkeiten geschaffen werden. Um ein konkretes persönliches Schicksal geht es nie. Die konsequente Beibehaltung ihrer Strategie der Gegenüberstellung bildhafter Zitate, bei deren zunehmender thematischer Bandbreite, ermöglicht es Petra Zimmermann, tableauartige Assemblagen zu entwerfen. So steht ein Halsschmuck von 2008 in der kunsthistorischen Tradition von Doppelportraits, wie etwa Warhols „Double Elvis" oder Jeff Walls „Double Self-Portrait". Beiden liegt die Frage nach den inhaltlichen

Petra Zimmermann does not use the combinations of quotations and her interpretations of jewellery from the perspective of cultural conventions to present mere clichés, in the sense of criticism of the artificial. On the contrary, her jewellery work – in paradoxical contrast to its aggressively opulent design – appears to serve as an unpretentious artistic medium that she can use to discuss themes that are relevant to the generation of younger artists. A generation for whom what really counts is no longer the fight against obsolete conventions but rather a search for personal and historical coherence in an ever more complex environment.

Halsschmuck | Necklace, 2008

Implikationen der medialen Doppelung einer Person zugrunde: bei Warhol die Doppelung des Abbildes der Popikone, bei Wall die Doppelung der eigenen Person. Zimmermann fügt in ihrem Halsschmuck eine Variante hinzu, indem sie die Abbilder zweier unterschiedlicher Models wählt, diese gleichberechtigt nebeneinanderstellt und spiegelbildlich jeweils mit identen Schmuck-Fragmenten versieht. Auf diese Weise scheint sie auf ein um den Hals getragenes Amulett zu referieren, das aufgeklappt ein Bild der/des Liebsten preisgibt. Die Doppelung der Schmuckattribute scheint so einerseits ironisch bildhaft auf so etwas wie genetische Verwandtschaft anzuspielen, aber andererseits mit ebenso ironischem Unterton auf die Lesbarkeit der Modelportraits zwar als unterschiedliche Erscheinung, jedoch mit einer „wesenhaften" Verwandtschaft zu verweisen.

Die Kombinationen der Zitate und ihre Interpretationen von Schmuck aus dem Blickwinkel kultureller Konvention benutzt Petra Zimmermann nicht, um bloße Klischees im Sinne einer Kritik am Falschen darzustellen. Vielmehr scheinen ihr die Schmuckarbeiten – in paradoxem Widerspruch zu ihrer offensiv-opulenten Ausformung – als unprätentiöses künstlerisches Medium zu dienen, mit dem sie die für die jüngere Künstlergeneration relevanten Themen diskutieren kann. Einer Generation, für die es nicht mehr zählt, gegen überkommene Konventionen anzukämpfen, sondern sich vielmehr in einer immer komplexeren Umwelt auf die Suche nach persönlicher und historischer Kohärenz zu begeben.

The Strategy of Artistic Appropriation
in the Jewellery of Petra Zimmermann

The Fascination of the Hybrid.

"...taking what is there and combining it."

Claude Lévi-Strauss, The Savage Mind

Reuse of materials has a long tradition in the history of jewellery. Even crown jewels were not safe against such disassembly – diamonds, emeralds and rubies were unceremoniously removed and re-set in new works, and the gold was melted down to finance wars or to be re-shaped for other purposes. Against this backdrop, the young Viennese jewellery artist Petra Zimmermann is not actually doing something unknown when she takes historical pieces and re-uses them to create something entirely her own. Nonetheless, her appropriations are made in a very different context. Whereas in earlier centuries gold-smiths' works were destroyed in order to plunder the precious materials of which they were made, Petra Zimmermann takes not the component material but the material ornament – the entire form or even the entire work along with all of its mechanical parts. Furthermore, most of her decorative pieces are found at flea markets and can generally be classified as historical fashion or art nouveau jewellery, and her work gives them a status that is not derived from their mere material value. And if this makes you think along the lines of pedestrian historicism, you are in for a pleasant surprise: Zimmermann's "jewellery within jewellery" pieces have an unmistakably youthful character. The main material that holds together her bricolages of times past is plastic, and her deliciously incongruous pieces by no means always adhere to conventional definitions of jewellery.

The rise of artistic avant-garde jewellery in the 1960s initiated a debate over the re-definition of jewellery, the possibility of broadening of the meaning of the term and the definition, and elimination, of the demarcation lines between jewellery and accessories, applied art and free art. These passionate altercations reached their high-point with the exhibition Schmuck – Zeichen am Körper (Jewellery – Symbols on the Body) in Linz in 1988, which declared everything worn on or near to the body to be potential jewellery.

Several generations later, Petra Zimmermann nonchalantly takes a little clutch with a chain-link strap, adds a large circular hole rimmed with plastic and applies some add-itional ornaments, including an historic brooch. What do we have as a result? Deprived of its original functionality by the rather brutal insertion of the circular torque, the clutch is definitely no longer an accessory. It is no longer possible to open it or put anything inside it. Could the strap now be a necklace and the clutch its pendant? Or is it a bag-armlet? It is. Surreal and yet eminently wearable, and highly decorative with its cleverly-applied belt buckles and brooches. All quite literally melted together to a unity in the crucible on the stove. And it is not only the individual components of different proven-ances and dates that have been fused together here – the same has happened to the associated concepts and categories: The bag has become an armlet, the belt buckle decorates the bag and the armlet and everything taken together decorates the wearer.

Zitat als künstlerische Strategie
im Schmuck von Petra Zimmermann

Die Faszination des Hybriden.

"...nehmen und verknüpfen was da ist."

Claude Lévi-Strauss, Das wilde Denken

Barbara Maas

In der Geschichte des Schmuckschaffens hat die Wiederverwertung schmuckhafter Materialien eine lange Tradition. Selbst vor Kronjuwelen machte die Demontage nicht halt, und so wurden Diamanten, Smaragde und Rubine herausgebrochen, um sie in neue Schmuckstücke einzusetzen und Gold eingeschmolzen, um Kriege zu finanzieren oder es anderen Gestaltungen zuzuführen. Mithin bedient sich die junge Wiener Schmuckkünstlerin Petra Zimmermann in ihrem Œuvre keiner völlig unbekannten Strategie, wenn sie sich historische Stücke aneignet und daraus Eigenes entstehen lässt. Allerdings finden ihre Appropriationen vor einem gänzlich anderen Hintergrund statt. Wurden in vergangenen Jahrhunderten Objekte der Goldschmiedekunst zerstört, um sich in plündernder Manier des kostbaren Materials zu bemächtigen, so übernimmt Petra Zimmermann nicht das Material, sondern das materielle Ornament, die ganze Schmuckform bzw. das Stück mitsamt seiner mechanischen Teile. Dabei stammen die meisten ihrer Zierstücke vom Flohmarkt und sind dem historischen Mode- oder dem Jugendstilschmuck zuzuordnen. Sie lässt ihnen eine Wertschätzung zuteilwerden, die sich nicht an ihrem Materialwert orientiert. Wer nun biederen Historismus befürchtet, wird angenehm überrascht. Die Zimmermannschen „Schmuck-im-Schmuck"-Stücke zeugen von unverkennbar jugendlichem Gestus. Und das zentrale Material, welches diese unbeschwerten Vergangenheits-Bricolagen zusammenhält, ist Kunststoff. Auch folgen die Versatzstücke keineswegs immer gängigen Definitionen von Schmuck.

Mit dem Auftauchen des künstlerischen Avantgardeschmucks in den 60er Jahren des 20. Jahrhunderts begann eine Diskussion über die Neudefinition des Schmuckes, die mögliche Erweiterung des Schmuckbegriffs und die Grenzziehungen bzw. -aufhebungen zwischen Schmuck und Accessoire, angewandter Kunst und freier Kunst. Die sehr leidenschaftlich geführten Auseinandersetzungen erreichten einen Höhepunkt mit der Ausstellung „Schmuck – Zeichen am Körper" in Linz 1988, die alles, was am oder in der Nähe des Körpers getragen wurde, als potentiellen Schmuck deklarierte.

Armreif | Bracelet, 2010

Einige Generationen später nimmt Petra Zimmermann nonchalant ein Abendtäschchen mitsamt seinem Trageriemen aus Kettengliedern, versieht es mit einem kreisrunden Loch aus Kunststoff und bestückt es mit zusätzlichen Ornamenten, z. B. einer historischen Brosche. Was haben wir denn hier? Seiner Funktionalität durch das etwas brachial anmutende Armreifrund beraubt, ist diese Tasche kein Accessoire mehr. Weder kann man sie öffnen, noch etwas hinein tun. Könnte der Trageriemen eine Kette sein, für die das Täschchen den Anhänger gibt? Oder ist es ein Taschen-Armreif? Es ist. Surrealistisch, dennoch eindeutig tragbar und hochgradig schmückend mit seinen geschickt applizierten Gürtelschnallen und Broschen. Alles buchstäblich zu einer Einheit miteinander ver-

Petra Zimmermann's work is "hybrid jewellery", a fascinating combination of jewellery forms, types, individual ornaments and entire styles. She even turns the mechanical components, like clasps and brooch pins, into jewellery elements, glittering seductively in their clear plastic, as though encased in crystal. These inspiring hybrid creations are ebulliently and delightfully sensual, lavish, extravagant, baroque, hedonist. And also saucy, carefree and luxurious, in a radical sense. And wild. Beautifully wild.

The Image behind the Image.

Exquisite detail, intense, luminous colours and alternation between two and three dimensionality are all prominent in the line of polymer brooches that Petra Zimmermann just recently added to her twelve-year oeuvre. As so often in her works, floral associations are also unavoidable – one feels intoxicated by the sensuous allure of exotic vegetation and lascivious jungle blossoms. It is hardly discernible that many of these opulent, glamorous and precious creations are actually based on commonplace photos of blossoms clipped from ordinary print media. This is hidden by the overpainting and extensive reworking of the image by the artist. Even in those works where the original motif is still clearly identifiable and does not have a floral origin, for example the brooch featuring a classic design by Harry Bertoia, Petra Zimmermann still reworks it in a way that transforms the represented object: Like the opening calyx of a blossom, it is transmuted attractively and stylishly into the third dimension – and thus a humble chair becomes a jewellery motif. Where the earlier works of the young Viennese painter and jewellery artist frequently featured the human form, often in the form of anonymous models on the catwalk and in rather pinup-like poses, her recent jewellery is more abstract, with multi-layered imagery – there is an image behind the image. The term "image" generally refers both to the image itself as a material object and also to the object represented, irrespective of the individual medium. In the 1990s, scholars started to refer to the rapid increase in the volume and cultural importance of images in the 20th century as the "iconic turn". Responding to the ubiquity of photography in modern life and the fact that it has only been accepted as an art form for a few decades, many contemporary artists have focused intensely on the medium – for example Gerhard Richter's paintings based on photographs, Sigmar Polke's raster images and Arnulf Rainer's overpainted images. In parallel to this development, photography has also been used in contemporary jewellery art since the 1970s, for example in Gijs Bakker's large-format laminations, Herman Hermsen's "image flood" necklaces and Bettina Speckner's nostalgic photographic engravings on zinc. Petra Zimmermann's approach is different: She overpaints and reworks the photographic image until it is almost unrecognisable; i.e. she superimposes a traditional painting or drawing over the technical image (the photograph). Furthermore, the images melted into the plastic of her pieces are neither well-known pictures by prominent art photographers, nor do they transport the heavy burden of reminiscences typical of family photos. They are unspectacular "found footage" – bulk goods, so to speak.
Petra Zimmermann's adoption of the images is preceded by de-contextualisation, which includes a removal of any intrinsic meaning: the image is converted to pure material. At

schmolzen im Schmelztiegel auf dem Herd. Und es sind nicht allein die Einzelteile unterschiedlicher Provenienz und Datierung, welche hier fusionieren: die Gattungsbegriffe tun es ebenso. So wird die Tasche zum Armreif, die Gürtelschnalle ziert das Täschchen und den Armreif und alles zusammen schmückt die Trägerin.

Petra Zimmermann schafft „Hybrid-Schmuck", faszinierende Vermischungen von Schmuckformen, Gattungen, einzelnen Ornamenten und ganzen Stilrichtungen. Auch die mechanischen Teile, wie Verschlüsse und Broschierungen, geraten bei ihr zum Schmuckelement und schimmern verführerisch, wie in Kristall eingeschlossen, im Kunststoff. Die so entstandenen inspirierenden Hybridschöpfungen sind sinnenfrohe und die Sinne erfreuende Stücke, verschwenderisch, extravagant, barock, hedonistisch. Keck auch, unbekümmert, auf radikale Art luxuriös. Und wild. Schön wild.

Das Bild hinter dem Bild.

Exquisite Detailliertheit und eine intensive, leuchtende Farbigkeit sind den zwischen Fläche und Räumlichkeit changierenden Kunststoffbroschen zu eigen, die Petra Zimmermann erst jüngst ihrem nunmehr seit zwölf Jahren gewachsenen Schmuckwerk hinzufügte. Wie häufig bei ihren Arbeiten drängen sich Assoziationen zu Floralem auf und man lässt sich vom sinnlichen Reiz exotischer Vegetation betören: laszive Dschungelblüten. Dass einer Reihe dieser üppigen, glamourösen und kostbaren Kunststoffkreationen banale Bilder von Blüten, ausgeschnitten aus Printmedien, zugrundeliegen, ist kaum noch erkennbar, handelt es sich hier doch um Bildübermalungen und extensive Bildbearbeitungen seitens der Künstlerin. Selbst dort, wo ein Motiv sich eindeutig zu erkennen gibt und nicht aus dem floralen Bereich entstammt, wie beispielsweise der Ansteckschmuck mit einem Design-Klassiker von Harry Bertoia, bearbeitet Petra Zimmermann es in einer Weise, die das abgebildete Objekt transformiert: Es schwingt sich einem Blütenkelch gleich verlockend und mondän in die dritte Dimension – ein Stuhl wird schmuckwürdig. Hatten frühere Arbeiten der jungen Wiener Malerin und Schmuckkünstlerin oftmals den menschlichen Körper zum Motiv, vorwiegend den anonymer Models auf dem Laufsteg oder in Pin-up-verdächtigen Posen, so ist der neue Schmuck abstrakter und von doppelter Bildlichkeit. Es gibt ein Bild hinter dem Bild. Der Begriff des Bildes bezeichnet gemeinhin sowohl den materiellen Gegenstand als auch den unabhängig vom Medium dargestellten Bildgegenstand. Angesichts der rapide gestiegenen Anzahl und kulturellen Bedeutung von Bildern im 20. Jahrhundert spricht man seit den 1990er Jahren in der Wissenschaft vom iconic turn. Insbesondere die Allgegenwart der Fotografie im modernen Leben und ihre vor erst wenigen Jahrzehnten erfolgte Anerkennung als kunstwürdig hat in der Gegenwartskunst zu einer ausführlichen Beschäftigung mit diesem Medium geführt, sei es in der 'Malerei nach der Fotografie' eines Gerhard Richter, den Rasterbildern Sigmar Polkes oder den Bild-Übermalungen von Arnulf Rainer. Analog zu dieser Entwicklung fand die Verwendung von Fotografien seit den 1970er Jahren auch Eingang in das zeitgenössische Schmuckschaffen, bei Gijs Bakkers großformatigen Laminierungen etwa, Herman Hermsens Ketten zum Thema Bilderflut oder Bettina Speckners nostalgisch anmutenden Fotoätzungen auf Zink. Petra Zimmermanns Herangehensweise jedoch ist eine andere: Sie übermalt und überarbeitet das fotografische Bild fast bis zur Unkenntlichkeit, d.h. sie

Brosche | Brooch, 2010

the same time, the selection and reworking of foreign, multi-medial "image noise" into the work results in a new image with strong associations. In the case of Petra Zimmermann, no conscious redefinition is inherent in these associations; there is plenty of room for interpretation. Photography is transformed into jewellery. The jewellery is an image.

Although many of Petra Zimmermann's jewellery works remain substantially two-dimensional, in keeping with their photographic origins, there are also many examples of powerful pictorial abstractions moving towards the three-dimensional. Complex structures created with layers and intersections of surfaces with contrasting designs create the impression of lush vegetation with brilliant colours and jewel-like effulgence, without a trace of the accompanying morbidity that one finds in Art Nouveau.

Although one can't help comparing these newer works with Art Nouveau, at least those that both evoke Nature associations and have titles explicitly referring to Nature themes, Zimmermann's jewellery is actually far removed from the stylised blossoms of Art Nouveau. It is not Nature that is the young jewellery artist's model but the reproduction of Nature; not the flower but the image of a flower. She develops her artistic strategies of overpainting and over-drawing on the basis of the image and with the image. Overpainting, in the sense of the technical term, has been used by artists since medieval times: In contrast to direct painting, this technique involves the application of layers of paint in which each layer has a reciprocally dependent relationship with the layer beneath it. Petra Zimmermann's works also communicate this multi-layered, multi-faceted impression. How deeply the wearer wishes to engage with this is left up to her own imagination. If she recognises the mass media image on which the work is based, she could actually find herself in an interesting dilemma: a contradiction between the depersonalisation expressed by the work and the emphasis of individuality inherent in jewellery as a medium. And this is ultimately the essence of artistic jewellery: It is unsettling, it raises questions and demands commitment on the part of the wearer. And if it also manages to be decorative and kindle desire, as Petra Zimmermann's works do, then there is nothing wrong with that – artistic quality does not exclude aesthetic quality.

legt über das technische Bild (Foto) ein traditionelles, nämlich das der Malerei oder der Zeichnung. Überdies sind die von ihr verwendeten, in Kunststoff eingeschmolzenen Bilder weder eminente Fotografien berühmter Fotokünstler noch transportieren sie die Last bedeutungsschwerer Erinnerungen von Familienfotos. Sie sind unspektakuläre Massenware, „found footage"-Material.

Der Aneignung der Bilder durch Petra Zimmermann geht eine Dekontextualisierung voraus, welche zunächst in eine Sinnentleerung mündet: Das Bild wird zum reinen Material. Gleichzeitig aber lässt die Auswahl und Bearbeitung fremder, dem massenmedialen Bilderrauschen entnommener Bildlichkeit ein neues, assoziationsstarkes Bild entstehen, welchem im Falle Petra Zimmermanns keine bewusste Umcodierung inhärent ist, aber Interpretationsspielraum. Die Fotografie wird zum Schmuck. Der Schmuck ist Bild.

Brosche | Brooch, 2010

Obwohl eine ganze Reihe der Zimmermannschen Schmuckstücke, der Fotografie folgend, in der Zweidimensionalität verharren, gibt es auch zahlreiche Beispiele für formstarke, ins Dreidimensionale gehende malerische Abstraktionen. Komplex aufgebaute Strukturen aus Schichtungen und Überkreuzungen differenziert gestalteter Oberflächen vermitteln ein Bild überbordender Vegetation von Juwelen gleichem Glanz und brillanter Farbigkeit, der – anders als im Jugendstil – jegliche Morbidität fernliegt.

Natürlich drängt sich dort, wo die neueren Arbeiten nicht nur Natur-Assoziationen evozieren, sondern auch in ihren Titeln explizit auf Natur rekurrieren, der Vergleich mit dem Jugendstil auf, von dessen stilisierten Blüten der Schmuck Petra Zimmermanns indes weit entfernt ist. Der jungen Schmuckkünstlerin dient nicht die Natur selber als Vorlage, sondern die reproduzierte Natur, nicht die Blume, sondern das Bild einer Blume. Mit ihm und auf ihm entwickelt sie ihre künstlerischen Strategien der Übermalung und Überzeichnung. „Übermalung" als Terminus technicus ist seit der im Mittelalter ausgeübten Schichtenmalerei bekannt. Im Gegensatz zur einschichtigen Primamalerei steht bei einem aus mehreren Malschichten aufgebauten Staffeleibild die Übermalung in einem reziproken Abhängigkeitsverhältnis zu ihrer jeweiligen Untermalung. Diesen Eindruck der Vielschichtigkeit vermitteln auch die Arbeiten Zimmermanns. Es bleibt der Fantasie der Trägerin überlassen, wie tief sie sich darauf einlässt. Erkennt sie das dem Schmuckstück zugrundeliegende Massenbild aus der Presse, könnte sie angesichts der hier praktizierten Entpersönlichung in einem auf die Betonung der Individualität zielenden Medium des Schmucks, in einen interessanten Zwiespalt geraten. Und dies macht den künstlerischen Schmuck schließlich aus: Er verunsichert, wirft Fragen auf, erfordert ein bekenntnishaftes Tragen. Wenn er zudem auch noch schmückt und Begehrlichkeit weckt, wie die Kreationen Petra Zimmermanns, ist das nicht verkehrt, denn künstlerische Qualität schließt ästhetische Qualität nicht aus.

2010–2009

History Repeating
New Works

Alle Schmuckstücke auf den Seiten 21–31, 34–45, 53–63, 71–87 sind +/- 10% der Originalgröße abgebildet
All pieces of jewellery on pages 21–31, 34–45, 53–63, 71–87 have been reproduced +/- 10% of their original size

Brosche, 2010, Polymethylmethacrylat, zerstoßene Perlen,
Strass, Rauchquarz, Lack, Blattgold, Silber geschwärzt
Brooch, 2010, polymethyl methacrylate, crushed pearls,
rhinestones, smoky quartz, lacquer, gold leaf, blackened silver
Privatsammlung/ *Private collection*

Armreif, 2010, historisches Abendtäschchen,
Polymethylmethacrylat, Silber, Messing, Stahl
*Bracelet, 2010, antique handbag,
polymethyl methacrylate, silver, brass, steel*

Brosche, 2010, Polymethylmethacrylat,
zerstoßene Perlen, Strass, Amethyste, Blatt-
Weißgold, Lack, Stahlseil, Silber geschwärzt
Brooch, 2010, polymethyl methacrylate,
crushed pearls, rhinestones, amethysts, white
gold leaf, lacquer, steel wire, blackened silver

Brosche, 2010, Bakelit, Rauchquarz,
Niello, Blattgold, Silber geschwärzt
Brooch, 2010, Bakelite, smoky quartz,
niello, gold leaf, blackened silver

Brosche „Bertoia Asymmetric Chaise I", 2010,
Polymethylmethacrylat, Obsidian-Perlen,
Niello, Blattgold, Silber geschwärzt
Brooch "Bertoia Asymmetric Chaise I", 2010,
polymethyl methacrylate, obsidian beads, niello,
gold leaf, blackened silver
Privatsammlung/*Private collection*

Brosche „Bertoia Asymmetric Chaise II", 2010,
Polymethylmethacrylat, Obsidian, Blattgold,
Silber geschwärzt
Brooch "Bertoia Asymmetric Chaise II", 2010,
polymethyl methacrylate, obsidian,
gold leaf, blackened silver
Privatsammlung/*Private collection*

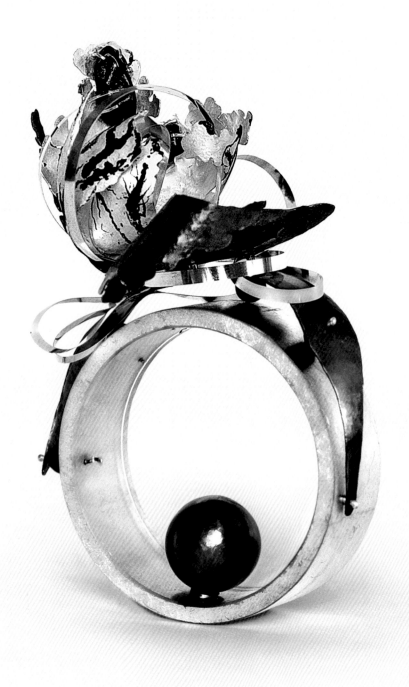

Brosche, 2010, Silber geschwärzt, Niello,
Chalzedon-Perlen, Mammut-Elfenbein
Brooch, 2010, blackened silver, niello,
chalcedony beads, mammouth ivory

Armreif, 2010, Polymethylmethacrylat, Niello,
Obsidian, Blatt-Weißgold, Silber teilweise geschwärzt
Bracelet, 2010, polymethyl methacrylate, niello,
obsidian, white gold leaf, partly blackened silver

Ring, 2010, Polymethylmethacrylat,
Silber geschwärzt
Ring, 2010, polymethyl methacrylate,
blackened silver

Ring, 2010, Vintage-Modeschmuck-
Halbzeug, Polymethylmethacrylat,
Obsidiane, Strass, Blattgold, Gold
*Ring, 2010, vintage costume jewellery
findings, polymethyl methacrylate,
obsidians, rhinestones, gold leaf, gold*

Armreif, 2010, historische Abendtasche (Alpaka),
Vintage-Modeschmuck, Polymethylmethacrylat,
Blattgold, Silber geschwärzt
*Bracelet, 2010, antique handbag (alpaca), vintage
costume jewellery, polymethyl methacrylate, gold leaf,
blackened silver*

Armreif, 2010, Vintage-Modeschmuck-Halbzeug,
Polymethylmethacrylat, Blatt-Weißgold, Obsidian,
Strass, Modelliermasse, Silber geschwärzt
Bracelet, 2010, vintage costume jewellery findings,
polymethyl methacrylate, white gold leaf, obsidian,
rhinestones, polymer clay, blackened silver

Brosche, 2010, Polymethylmethacrylat,
zerstoßene Perlen, Onyx-Perlen,
Blatt-Weißgold, Niello, Silber geschwärzt
Brooch, 2010, polymethyl methacrylate,
crushed pearls, onyx beads, white gold leaf,
niello, blackened silver

Ring, 2010, Vintage-Modeschmuck-
Halbzeug, Polymethylmethacrylat,
Granate, Strass, Lack, Blattgold, Gold
*Ring, 2010, vintage costume jewellery
findings, polymethyl methacrylate,
garnets, rhinestones, lacquer, gold leaf, gold*

Ring, 2010, Vintage-Modeschmuck,
Polymethylmethacrylat, Lack, Gold
*Ring, 2010, vintage costume jewellery,
polymethyl methacrylate, lacquer, gold*

Ring, 2009, Teile von Vintage-Modeschmuck, Polymethylmethacrylat, Blattgold, Gold
Ring, 2009, various parts of vintage costume jewellery, polymethyl methacrylate, gold leaf, gold

Doppelring, 2009, Vintage-Brosche, Polymethylmethacrylat, Blattgold, Gold
Double ring, 2009, vintage brooch, polymethyl methacrylate, gold leaf, gold

Ring, 2009, Vintage-Brosche, Polymethylmethacrylat, Blattgold, Gold
Ring, 2009, vintage brooch, polymethyl methacrylate, gold leaf, gold

Ring, 2009, Vintage-Brosche, Polymethylmethacrylat, Blatt-Weißgold, Gold
*Ring, 2009, vintage brooch, polymethyl
methacrylate, white gold leaf, gold*
Privatsammlung/*Private collection*

Ring, 2010, Vintage-Brosche, Polymethylmethacrylat, Bernstein, Strass, Blattgold, Gold
*Ring, 2010, vintage brooch, polymethyl methacrylate,
amber, rhinestones, gold leaf, gold*

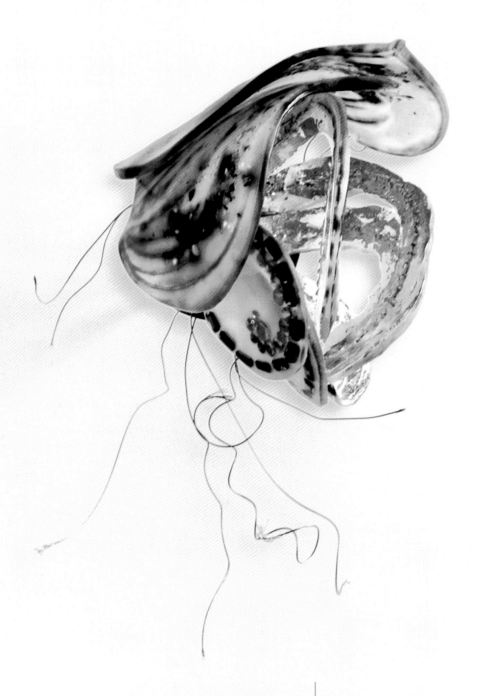

Brosche, 2010, Polymethylmethacrylat,
zerstoßene Perlen, Strass, Lack, Stahlseil,
Blattgold, Silber geschwärzt
*Brooch, 2010, polymethyl methacrylate,
crushed pearls, rhinestones, lacquer,
steel wire, gold leaf, blackened silver*

Brosche, 2010, Polymethylmethacrylat, Niello,
Blattgold, Feingold, Silber geschwärzt
*Brooch, 2010, polymethyl methacrylate,
niello, gold leaf, fine gold, blackened silver*

Kette mit Anhänger, 2009,
Polymethylmethacrylat,
Blattgold, Silber geschwärzt
Necklace with pendant, 2009,
polymethyl methacrylate,
gold leaf, blackened silver

Halsschmuck „*Two Portraits*", 2009, Polymethylmethacrylat,
Vintage-Gürtelschnalle (Cut-Steel-Imitation), Acrylfarbe,
Blatt-Weißgold, Silber geschwärzt
Necklace "Two Portraits", 2009, polymethyl methacrylate,
vintage belt buckle (imitation cut steel), acrylic paint,
white gold leaf, blackened silver

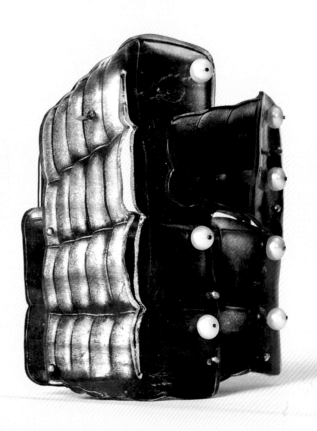

Brosche, 2009, Polymethylmethacrylat,
Perle, Blatt-Weißgold, Silber geschwärzt
Brooch, 2009, polymethyl methacrylate,
pearl, white gold leaf, blackened silver
Privatsammlung/*Private collection*

Brosche „KUBUS", 2009,
Polymethylmethacrylat, Perlen,
Blatt-Weißgold, Silber geschwärzt
Brooch "KUBUS", 2009,
polymethyl methacrylate, pearls,
white gold leaf, blackened silver
Privatsammlung/*Private collection*

Armreif, 2009, Vintage-Modeschmuck-Halbzeug,
Polymethylmethacrylat, Strass, Kieselsteine, Blattgold
Bracelet, 2009, vintage costume jewellery findings,
polymethyl methacrylate, rhinestones, pebbles, gold leaf

Armreif, 2010, Vintage-Modeschmuck-
Halbzeug, Polymethylmethacrylat,
Strass, Obsidian, Lack, Blattgold
Bracelet, 2010, vintage costume jewellery
findings, polymethyl methacrylate,
rhinestones, obsidian, lacquer, gold leaf

Armreif, 2009, Vintage-Modeschmuck-
Halbzeug, Polymethylmethacrylat,
Strass, Obsidian, Blattgold
Bracelet, 2009, vintage costume jewellery
findings, polymethyl methacrylate,
rhinestones, obsidian, gold leaf

Brosche „Tom Ford Flagship Store NY", 2007, Polymethylmethacrylat, Rauchquarz, Blattgold, Messing vergoldet
*Brooch "Tom Ford Flagship Store NY", 2007, polymethyl
methacrylate, smoky quartz, gold leaf, gilded brass*
Privatsammlung/ *Private collection*

Brosche, 2009, Polymethylmethacrylat,
Rutilquarz, Blatt-Weißgold, Silber geschwärzt
*Brooch, 2009, polymethyl methacrylate,
rutile, white gold leaf, blackened silver*
Privatsammlung/ *Private collection*

Objekt „LINGAM II", 2009,
Polymethylmethacrylat, Vintage-
Modeschmuck-Halbzeug, Lack,
Blattgold, Silber geschwärzt
*Object "LINGAM II", 2009,
polymethyl methacrylate, vintage
costume jewellery findings, lacquer,
gold leaf, blackened silver*

Kette, 2009, Polymethylmethacrylat, Bakelit, Silber
Necklace, 2009, polymethyl methacrylate, Bakelite, silver

Armreif, 2009, Vintage-
Modeschmuck-Halbzeug,
Polymethylmethacrylat, Strass,
Kieselsteine, Blattgold
*Bracelet, 2009, vintage
costume jewellery findings,
polymethyl methacrylate,
rhinestones, pebbles, gold leaf*

Ring, 2009, Vintage-Modeschmuck-
Halbzeug, Polymethylmethacrylat,
Strass, Blattgold, Silber geschwärzt
*Ring, 2009, vintage costume jewellery
findings, polymethyl methacrylate,
rhinestones, gold leaf, blackened silver*

2008–2006

Off the Wall

Brosche, 2007, Polymethylmethacrylat, Druckfarbe,
Perlen, Blattgold, Blatt-Weißgold, Silber geschwärzt
Brooch, 2007, polymethyl methacrylate, printing ink,
pearls, gold leaf, white gold leaf, blackened silver

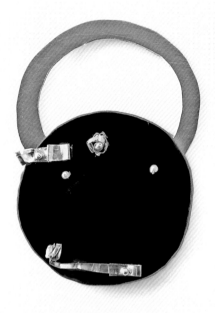

Ohrschmuck, 2007, Acrylglas,
Feingold, Silber geschwärzt
Earrings, 2007, acrylic glass,
fine gold, blackened silver

Brosche „Pelzmantel", 2007, Polymethylmethacrylat,
Druckfarbe, Goldfluss, Blattgold, Gold, Silber geschwärzt
Brooch "Fur Coat", 2007, polymethyl methacrylate,
printing ink, goldstone, gold leaf, gold, blackened silver
Privatsammlung/ *Private collection*

Skizzen für Halsschmuck, 2008, Collagen
Sketches for necklaces, 2008, collages

Halsschmuck, 2008, Polymethylmethacrylat, Druckfarbe,
zerstoßene Perlen, Onyx-Perlen, Blatt-Weißgold, Silber geschwärzt
*Necklace, 2008, polymethyl methacrylate, printing ink, crushed pearls,
onyx beads, white gold leaf, blackened silver*
Privatsammlung/*Private collection*

Brosche „Schwarzer Mantel", 2008, Polymethylmethacrylat, Druckfarbe, Vintage-Modeschmuck-
Halbzeug, Perlen, Bergkristall-, Onyx- und Glas-Perlen,
Blatt-Weißgold, Silber geschwärzt
*Brooch "Black Coat", 2008, polymethyl methacrylate,
printing ink, vintage costume jewellery findings, pearls,
crystal, onyx and glass beads, white gold leaf, blackened silver*

Armreif, 2008, Vintage-Broschen,
Polymethylmethacrylat, Lack, Blattgold
*Bracelet, 2008, vintage brooches, polymethyl
methacrylate, lacquer, gold leaf*

Drei Armreifen, 2006 (im Vordergrund),
2007, 2008 (im Hintergrund),
Polymethylmethacrylat, Blattgold
*Three bracelets, 2006 (in the foreground),
2007, 2008 (in the background), polymethyl
methacrylate, gold leaf*

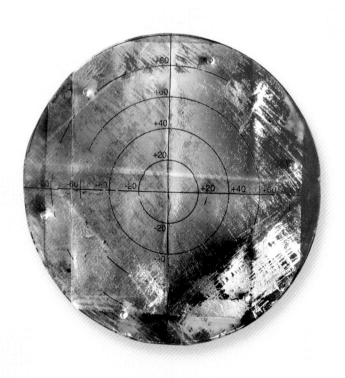

Brosche, 2009, Polymethylmethacrylat, Vintage-Schmuck,
Druckfarbe, Acrylglas, Blattgold, Silber geschwärzt
*Brooch, 2009, polymethyl methacrylate, vintage jewellery,
printing ink, acrylic glass, gold leaf, blackened silver*
Privatsammlung/ *Private collection*

Brosche „CMYK III", 2007, Polymethylmethacrylat,
Druckfarbe, Granate, Blattgold, Silber geschwärzt
*Brooch "CMYK III", 2007, polymethyl methacrylate,
printing ink, garnets, gold leaf, blackened silver*

Brosche, 2007, Polymethylmethacrylat,
Rauchquarz-Perlen, Druckfarbe,
Blattgold, Messing vergoldet
*Brooch, 2007, polymethyl methacrylate,
smoky quartz beads, printing ink,
gold leaf, gilded brass*
Privatsammlung/ *Private collection*

Brosche „Pyramide", 2007,
Messing vergoldet, Amethyst-Perlen
Brooch "Pyramid", 2007,
gilded brass, amethyst beads
Privatsammlung/ *Private collection*

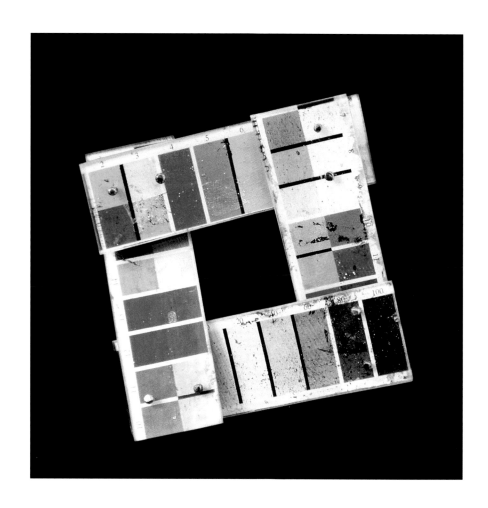

Fragment, 1997, Silber
Fragment, 1997, silver

Brosche „64 Colours", 2007, Polymethylmethacrylat,
Druckfarbe, Lack, Blatt-Weißgold, Silber geschwärzt
Brooch "64 Colours", 2007, polymethyl methacrylate,
printing ink, lacquer, white gold leaf, blackened silver
Privatsammlung/*Private collection*

Ring, 2007, Vintage-Brosche, Polymethylmethacrylat, Lack, Gold
Ring, 2007, vintage brooch, polymethyl methacrylate, lacquer, gold
Privatsammlung/ *Private collection*

2005–2003

Cut-Outs and Pin-Ups

Brosche „Pin-Up VI", 2004, Polymethylmethacrylat, Strass, Onyx-Perlen, Pyrite, Blattgold, Gold, Silber geschwärzt
Brooch "Pin-Up VI", 2004, polymethyl methacrylate, rhinestones, onyx beads, pyrites, gold leaf, gold, blackened silver

Brosche „Aulandschaft", 2007,
Polymethylmethacrylat, Brosche,
Hirschknopf, Druckfarbe,
Onyx-Perlen, Blattgold, Silber
*Brooch "Meadow", 2007, polymethyl
methacrylate, brooch, staghorn button,
printing ink, onyx beads, gold leaf, silver*
Privatsammlung/ *Private collection*

Brosche „Atomic Blast", 2005,
Strass, Niello, Silber geschwärzt
Brooch "Atomic Blast", 2005,
rhinestones, niello, blackened silver
Privatsammlung/*Private collection*

Brosche, 2005, Pyrite, Blatt-Weißgold, Niello, Silber geschwärzt
Brooch, 2005, pyrites, white gold leaf, niello, blackened silver

Brosche, 2003, Niello,
Silber geschwärzt
Brooch, 2003, niello,
blackened silver
Privatsammlung/ *Private collection*

Brosche „Important Meeting", 2003, Polymethylmethacrylat, Strass, Blattgold, Silber geschwärzt
Brooch "Important Meeting", 2003, polymethyl methacrylate,
rhinestones, gold leaf, blackened silver
Privatsammlung/ *Private collection*

Brosche „Pin-Up XII", 2005,
Perlen, Pyrite, Silber geschwärzt
Brooch "Pin-Up XII", 2005,
pearls, pyrites, blackened silver

Armreif, 2003, Polymethylmethacrylat, Blattgold
Bracelet, 2003, polymethyl methacrylate, gold leaf
Privatsammlung/ *Private collection*

Brosche „Diva I", 2003, Polymethylmethacrylat,
Strass, Perlmutt, Blattgold, Silber geschwärzt
Brooch "Diva I", 2003, polymethyl methacrylate,
rhinestones, mother of pearl, gold leaf, blackened silver
Privatsammlung/ *Private collection*

Armreif, 2003, Polymethylmethacrylat,
Vintage-Brosche, Blattgold
Bracelet, 2003, polymethyl methacrylate,
vintage brooch, gold leaf
Privatsammlung/ *Private collection*

Ring, 2004, Polymethylmethacrylat, Niello, Gold
Ring, 2004, polymethyl methacrylate, niello, gold

Ring, 2004, Polymethylmethacrylat, Niello, Silber geschwärzt
Ring, 2004, polymethyl methacrylate, niello, blackened silver
Privatsammlung/ *Private collection*

Ring, 2006, Polymethylmethacrylat, Niello, Silber geschwärzt
Ring, 2006, polymethyl methacrylate, niello, blackened silver

Ring, 2004, Polymethylmethacrylat, Pyrite, Niello, Silber geschwärzt
Ring, 2004, polymethyl methacrylate, pyrites, niello, blackened silver

Ring, 2006, Polymethylmethacrylat, Niello, Silber geschwärzt
Ring, 2006, polymethyl methacrylate, niello, blackened silver
Privatsammlung/ *Private collection*

2002–1998

Glamourös
Schmuck im Schmuck
Vorher – Nachher

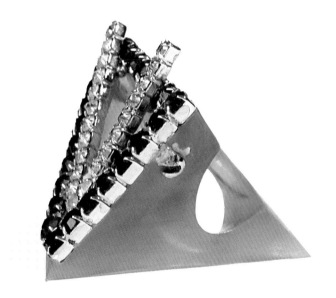

Ring, 2001, Vintage-Brosche, Polymethylmethacrylat
Ring, 2001, vintage brooch, polymethyl methacrylate

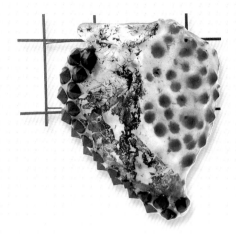

Brosche „Herz III", 2000, Polymethylmethacrylat, Strass, Blattgold, Messing vergoldet
*Brooch "Heart III", 2000, polymethyl
methacrylate, rhinestones, gold leaf, gilded brass*

Brosche „Herz V", 2000, Polymethylmethacrylat, Strass, Blattgold, Messing vergoldet
*Brooch "Heart V", 2000, polymethyl
methacrylate, rhinestones, gold leaf, gilded brass*

Brosche „Herz VI", 2000, Polymethylmethacrylat,
Strass, Blattgold, Messing vergoldet
*Brooch "Heart VI", 2000, polymethyl methacrylate,
rhinestones, gold leaf, gilded brass*

Brosche „Herz IV", 2000, Polymethylmethacrylat,
Strass, Blattgold, Messing vergoldet
*Brooch "Heart IV", 2000, polymethyl methacrylate,
rhinestones, gold leaf, gilded brass*

Brosche „Herz II", 2000, Polymethylmethacrylat,
Strass, Blattgold, Messing vergoldet
*Brooch "Heart II", 2000, polymethyl methacrylate,
rhinestones, gold leaf, gilded brass*
MAK, Wien/*Vienna*

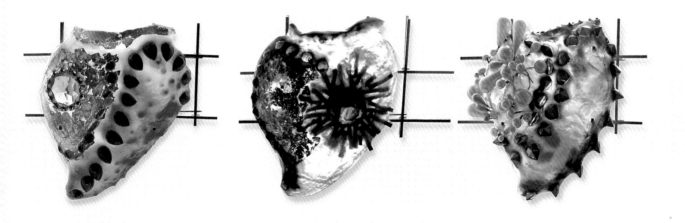

Ring „1. Preis", 1998, Teil eines Ordens, Silber
Ring "1. Preis", 1998, part of a medal, silver

Ring, 1998, Vintage-Gürtelschnalle, Silber vergoldet, Gold
Ring, 1998, vintage belt buckle, silver-gilt, gold

Ring, 1999, Vintage-Brosche, Polymethylmethacrylat, Gold
Ring, 1999, vintage brooch, polymethyl methacrylate, gold

Armreif, 1998, Vintage-Gürtelschnalle,
Polymethylmethacrylat, Edelstahl
*Bracelet, 1998, vintage belt buckle,
polymethyl methacrylate, stainless steel*

Ring, 1999, Polymethylmethacrylat, Vintage-Brosche, Gold
Ring, 1999, polymethyl methacrylate, vintage brooch, gold

Ring, 2002, Rauchquarz, Gold
Ring, 2002, smoky quartz, gold

Ring, 1998, Ring, Polymethylmethacrylat, Obsidian, Edelstahl
Ring, 1998, ring, polymethyl methacrylate, obsidian, stainless steel

Ring, 1998, Ring, Polymethylmethacrylat, Gold
Ring, 1998, ring, polymethyl methacrylate, gold

Ring, 1998, Polymethylmethacrylat, Goldketterl mit Perlenanhänger, Gold
Ring, 1998, polymethyl methacrylate, golden chain with pearl pendant, gold

Ring, 1998, Ring, Polymethylmethacrylat, Granate, Silber geschwärzt
Ring, 1998, ring, polymethyl methacrylate, garnets, blackened silver

Ring, 1998, Vintage-Anhänger, Polymethylmethacrylat, Gold
Ring, 1998, vintage pendant, polymethyl methacrylate, gold

Ring, 2000, Markesit-Brosche,
Polymethylmethacrylat, Silber geschwärzt
Ring, 2000, marcasite brooch,
polymethyl methacrylate, blackened silver

Fingerspange, 1999, Vintage-Brosche,
Polymethylmethacrylat
Ring, 1999, vintage brooch,
polymethyl methacrylate
Privatsammlung/ *Private collection*

Dieser Schmuck weiß, dass es Gucci gibt.
Und Quentin Tarantino.

Anna Schetelich
Mitarbeit:
Markus Böttcher

Petra Zimmermann bewegt sich mit traumwandlerischer Sicherheit in der Epoche der Wiener Secession, im Glamour der Hollywooddiven und im bildergefluteten Jetzt. Ihre Schmuckarbeiten schöpfen immer aus dem Leben – in all ihrer Haptik, ihrer Bildstärke und ihrer offensiven Sinnlichkeit. Vital und dialogisch beziehen sie sich immer auf ein Gegenüber als Voraussetzung aller Kommunikation.
Mit diesem offenen Blick in die Welt entsteht etwas souverän Eigenständiges.

Entsprechend enthusiastisch reagiert das Publikum: intuitiv, überrascht, überzeugt – auch Menschen, die sich eher wenig mit der Ästhetik des Glamours identifizieren.

Als ich Petra Zimmermanns Schmuck vor zehn Jahren zum ersten Mal begegnete, faszinierte und irritierte mich dessen neuartige, selbstbewusste Sprache sofort.
Ein Ensemble großformatiger Kunststoffarmreifen positionierte sich vollkommen gegensätzlich zum in der Kunstszene damals gefeierten Purismus, etwa der Mode eines Helmut Lang oder der Architektur eines Peter Zumthor: Prächtig funkelnde Strassbroschen, Originale aus der Ära des Filmdivenglamours, waren in transluzente Kunststoffkörper eingearbeitet; Broschen saßen Insekten gleich auf einem bonbonfarbenen mächtigen Armreif.
Die kritische Auseinandersetzung der Schmuckkünstler mit tradierten Vorstellungen von Schmuck, ihr Kampf, Autorenschmuck als Kunstform zu etablieren, all das schien diese Künstlerin wenig zu kümmern.

Quentin Tarantino sampelt unbekümmert trashige Comics und den europäischen Kunstfilm. Sein Publikum versteht seinen Overkill an Codes, Klischees und Kinozitaten und liebt ihn dafür. Seine Filme bilden die DNA für eine ganze Generation von Kreativen. Der permanente Ausnahmezustand ist für sie gefühlter Standard. Petra Zimmermanns Arbeiten reflektieren dieses Grundrauschen.
Prächtiger Dekolleté-Schmuck, das Gesicht einrahmende Ohrclips und funkelnde Armreifen haben das Bild der Filmdiven Hollywoods im Zusammenspiel mit Mode, Frisur und Make-up kreiert. Die Ästhetik dieser Diven schließt jede Intellektualität aus. Petra Zimmermann thematisiert die Omnipräsenz des „schönen Scheins". Ein wohldosiertes Übermaß an Blattgold, Strass und Bijouterie, das Glitzernde, Schimmernde, Opulente in ihren Schmuckarbeiten, diese ironisch übersteigerte Dekorationswut – durch permanente Überdehnung erschafft sie eine Doppelhelix aus unbewusster Faszination und sehr bewusster Reflexion.

Für Puristen bewegt sich Petra Zimmermann an einer Schmerzgrenze. Genau diese Schmerzgrenze gehört jedoch wesentlich zum ästhetischen Konzept der Künstlerin.
Und doch funktionieren am Ende alle ihre Arbeiten als Schmuck. So ist z.B. der skulpturale Charakter der Ringe und Armreifen stark körperbezogen und animiert ganz einfach zum Tragen.

This Jewellery knows Gucci.
And Quentin Tarantino.

Petra Zimmermann moves with equally consummate confidence in the epoch of the Vienna Secession, the glamour of Hollywood divas and the image-engulfed world of Now. Her jewellery work always draws on life – with all of its haptic immediacy, visual power and offensive sensuality. Vital and dialogue-engaged, her pieces always refer to an Other as the foundation of all communication. The result of this open view of the world is confident and individual.

Anna Schetelich
Contribution:
Markus Böttcher

Her audience responds with matching enthusiasm: intuitively touched, surprised, impressed – and this also applies for people who tend to feel less closely identified with the aesthetics of glamour.

When I encountered Petra Zimmermann's jewellery for the first time ten years ago, I was immediately fascinated and confounded by its novel and self-possessed language. She presented an ensemble of large-format plastic bracelets that were diametrically opposed to the purism that was then being celebrated in the art scene, for example in the fashion of Helmut Lang or the architecture of Peter Zumthor: Petra Zimmermann cast brilliantly glittering rhinestone brooches – original pieces from the era of film diva glamour – in forms of translucent plastic, placed brooches like insects on chunky, candy-coloured plastic bracelets. It seemed that this was an artist who was hardly concerned about art jewellery's normally critical approach to the traditional concepts of jewellery or the struggle to establish author jewellery as an art form.

Quentin Tarantino unashamedly samples trashy comics and European art cinema. His audience understands his overkill of codes, clichés and movie references and loves him for it. His movies have become the DNA for an entire generation of creative talents. For them, a permanent state of emergency is a subjective standard, and this background noise is reflected in Petra Zimmermann's works.
Magnificent décolleté-adorning necklaces, face-framing clip earrings and glittering bracelets all contributed to the creation of the image of Hollywood's film divas, supported by fashion, hairstyling and makeup. The aesthetics of these divas completely preclude any kind of intellectualism. Petra Zimmermann thematises the omnipresence of "beautiful appearances". In her work she creates a double helix of unconscious fascination and very conscious reflection with a judicious excess of gold leaf, rhinestones and costume jewellery elements, and with glitter, shimmer, opulence, ironically exaggerated decoration and continuous overreaching.

For purists, Petra Zimmermann operates at the very limit of the tolerable – and it is precisely this limit that is one of the key elements of the artist's aesthetic concept. Ultimately, however, all her pieces really do work as jewellery. For example, the sculptural character of her rings and bracelets is very body-oriented and quite simply makes you want to put them on.

In „Cut-outs and Pin-Ups", einer Serie von Broschen und Anhängern, akzentuiert Petra Zimmermann statt des Schmuckmaterials selbst die standardisierte Bilderwelt der Lifestyle-Magazine. Fotos von Models, Pin-up-Girls und Sportlern – für den schnellen Konsum bestimmte Bilder – werden der alltäglichen Bilderflut entrissen und konserviert. Technisch ausgedrückt werden sie in Kunststoff übertragen und mit Bijouterie-Fragmenten verschmolzen. Zusätzlich mit Blattgold hinterlegt, erfahren diese Figuren eine ungeahnte, oszillierende Ästhetik: Sie erscheinen als moderne Ikonen.

Möglicherweise lebt auch der moderne, aufgeklärt-abgeklärte Mensch permanent im Abgleich mit dem Koordinatensystem solcher Bildwelten, weit umfassender, als es ihm im Alltag zu Bewusstsein gelangen könnte.

„Cut-outs and Pin-Ups" erfährt eine Erweiterung in einer Serie mit Orchideen, Lilien und Kamelien. Diese Blumensujets spannen einen weiter gefassten Bogen als die Mädchen aus den Magazinen: Orchideen stehen für Schönheit, Sex und Tod.

Petra Zimmermann findet für eine Welt im permanenten Overkill, in der Bilder schnell verdichtet werden und ganz schnell wieder verglühen, eine adäquate Dramaturgie.

Bei aller Ironie ist jedes einzelne Schmuckstück jedoch vor allem ein Bekenntnis zum menschlichen Sein.

In "Cut-Outs and Pin-Ups", a series of brooches and pendants, Petra Zimmermann emphasises the standardised imagery of lifestyle magazines rather than the jewellery material. Photos of models, pin-up girls and athletes – pictures intended for fast consumption – are taken out of the everyday flow of images and conserved. In practice, this involves transferring them to plastic and casting them in it together with jewellery fragments. With additional gold leaf backing, these figures take on an unexpected, oscillating aesthetic quality, becoming modern icons. It is possible that hip, world-wise modern people are actually constantly aligning themselves with the coordinate systems defined by the world of images like these – to a much greater extent than they can ever be aware in their everyday lives.

"Cut-Outs and Pin-Ups" is further extended in a series that includes orchids, lilies and camellias. These floral motifs cover an even broader spectrum then the images of girls taken from magazines: orchids symbolise beauty, sex and death.

Petra Zimmermann has found an appropriate dramaturgy for a world in a state of permanent overkill, in which images are concentrated very fast only to fade just as quickly. Despite all the irony, however, every one of her jewellery pieces is also an homage to the human condition.

S. 93: Armreif, 1999, Polymethylmethacrylat,
Vintage-Gürtelschnallen
p. 93: Bracelet, 1999, polymethyl methacrylate,
vintage belt buckles

Ring, 2000, Vintage-Brosche,
Polymethylmethacrylat, Gold
*Ring, 2000, vintage brooch,
polymethyl methacrylate, gold*
Privatsammlung/*Private collection*

2010–1998

Arbeiten (in Auswahl)
Selected Works

001

002

003

004

005

006

001 Armreif, 2010, historisches Abendtäschchen, Polymethylmethacrylat, Silber,
Messing, Stahl
001 Bracelet, 2010, antique handbag,
polymethyl methacrylate, silver, brass, steel
140 x 127 x 60 mm

002 Ausstellungsansicht „History Repeating II",
Ornamentum Gallery, Hudson, NY 2010
002 Exhibition view "History Repeating II",
Ornamentum Gallery, Hudson, NY 2010

003 Kamm, 2010, Druckfarbe, Polymethylmethacrylat, Perle, Blattgold, Gold
003 Comb, 2010, printing ink, polymethyl
methacrylate, pearl, gold leaf, gold
152 x 135 x 25 mm

004 Ring, 2010, Vintage-Brosche,
Polymethylmethacrylat, Lack, Gold
004 Ring, 2010, vintage brooch,
polymethyl methacrylate, lacquer, gold
45 x 50 x 35 mm

005 Kette mit Anhänger „Camellia", 2010,
Polymethylmethacrylat, Strass, Blattgold,
Silber geschwärzt
005 Necklace with pendant "Camellia", 2010,
polymethyl methacrylate, rhinestones, gold leaf,
blackened silver
Anhänger/*Pendant:* 105 x 100 x 40 mm

006 Doppelring, 2010, Vintage-Modeschmuck-Halbzeug, Polymethylmethacrylat,
Granate, Strass, Blattgold, Gold
006 Double ring, 2010, vintage costume
jewellery findings, polymethyl methacrylate,
garnets, rhinestones, gold leaf, gold
50 x 68 x 46 mm
Privatsammlung/*Private collection*

007

008

009

010

011

012

007 Ausstellungsansicht „History Repeating II",
Ornamentum Gallery, Hudson, NY 2010
*007 Exhibition view "History Repeating II",
Ornamentum Gallery, Hudson, NY 2010*

008 Armreif „conglomerate", 2010, Vintage-
Modeschmuck-Halbzeug, Acrylglas, Blattgold,
Silber geschwärzt
*008 Bracelet „conglomerate", 2010, vintage
costume jewellery findings, acrylic glass, gold leaf,
blackened silver*
124 x 80 x 54 mm

009· Armreif, 2010, Vintage-Modeschmuck-
Halbzeug, Modelliermasse, Lack, Acrylglas,
Blattgold, Silber geschwärzt
*009 Bracelet, 2010, vintage costume jewellery
findings, polymer clay, lacquer, acrylic glass,
gold leaf, blackened silver*
120 x 120 x 58 mm

010 Ring, 2010, Vintage-Brosche,
Polymethylmethacrylat, Lack, Gold
*010 Ring, 2010, vintage brooch,
polymethyl methacrylate, lacquer, gold*
45 x 45 x 40 mm

011 Ring, 2010, Vintage-Broschen,
Polymethylmethacrylat, Gold
*011 Ring, 2010, vintage brooches,
polymethyl methacrylate, gold*
46 x 52 x 50 mm

012 Ausstellungsansicht „History Repeating II",
Ornamentum Gallery, Hudson, NY 2010
*012 Exhibition view "History Repeating II",
Ornamentum Gallery, Hudson, NY 2010*

013

014

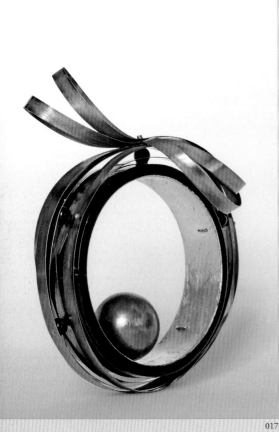

015

016

017

018

013 Brosche, 2010, Polymethylmethacrylat,
zerstoßene Perlen, Perlen, Glasperlen, Strass,
Lack, Blattgold, Silber geschwärzt
*013 Brooch, 2010, polymethyl methacrylate,
crushed pearls, pearls, glass beads, rhinestones,
lacquer, gold leaf, blackened silver*
120 x 115 x 62 mm

014 Brosche, 2010, Polymethylmethacrylat,
zerstoßene Perlen, Strass, Lack, Blattgold,
Silber geschwärzt
*014 Brooch, 2010, polymethyl methacrylate,
crushed pearls, rhinestones, lacquer, gold leaf,
blackened silver*
115 x 76 x 70 mm
Privatsammlung/ *Private collection*

015 Brosche, 2010, Silber geschwärzt,
Niello, Perlen, Blatt-Weißgold
*015 Brooch, 2010, blackened silver,
niello, pearls, white gold leaf*
78 x 70 x 18 mm

016 Ausstellungsansicht „History Repeating",
Galerie Biró, München 2010
*016 Exhibition view "History Repeating",
Galerie Biró, Munich 2010*

017 Armreif, 2010, Polymethylmethacrylat,
Blattgold, Silber geschwärzt
*017 Bracelet, 2010, polymethyl methacrylate,
gold leaf, blackened silver*
117 x 95 x 57 mm

018 Brosche, 2010, Polymethylmethacrylat,
Druckfarbe, Perlen, Obsidian-Perlen, Stahlseil,
Blattgold, Silber geschwärzt
*018 Brooch, 2010, polymethyl methacrylate,
printing ink, pearls, obsidian beads, steel wire,
gold leaf, blackened silver*
95 x 73 x 64 mm

019

020

021

022

023

024

019–021 Ausstellungsansichten „History Repeating", Galerie Biró, München 2010
019–021 Exhibition views "History Repeating", Galerie Biró, Munich 2010

022 Brosche, 2010, Polymethylmethacrylat, zerstoßene Perlen, Amethyst-Perlen, Strass, Lack, Blattgold, Silber geschwärzt
022 Brooch, 2010, polymethyl methacrylate, crushed pearls, amethyst beads, rhinestones, lacquer, gold leaf, blackened silver
80 x 70 x 85 mm
Privatsammlung/ *Private collection*

023 Ring, 2009, Cut-Steel-Schuhschnalle, Polymethylmethacrylat, Obsidian, Gold
023 Ring, 2009, cut steel shoe buckle, polymethyl methacrylate, obsidian, gold
38 x 50 x 29 mm

024 Ring, 2010, Cut-Steel-Schuhschnalle, Polymethylmethacrylat, Obsidian, Blatt-Weißgold, Silber
024 Ring, 2010, cut steel shoe buckle, polymethyl methacrylate, obsidian, white gold leaf, silver
40 x 49 x 28 mm

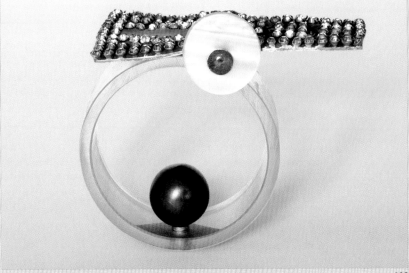

025

026

027–028

029

030

025 Armreif, 2009, Vintage-Modeschmuck-Halbzeug, Modelliermasse, Blattgold, Silber geschwärzt
025 Bracelet, 2009, vintage costume jewellery findings, polymer clay, gold leaf, blackened silver
115 x 102 x 50 mm

026 Objekt „LINGAM II", 2009, Polymethylmethacrylat, Vintage-Modeschmuck-Halbzeug, Lack, Blattgold, Silber geschwärzt
026 Object "LINGAM II", 2009, polymethyl methacrylate, vintage costume jewellery findings, lacquer, gold leaf, blackened silver
h. 170 mm, dm. 55 mm

027 Brosche, 2009, Vintage-Brosche, Poly-methylmethacrylat, Rauchquarz, Granate, Amethyst-Perlen, Blattgold, Gold, Silber geschwärzt
027 Brooch, 2009, vintage brooch, polymethyl methacrylate, smoky quartz, garnets, amethyst beads, gold leaf, gold, blackened silver
106 x 80 x 47 mm

028 Brosche, 2009, Polymethylmethacrylat, Onyx-Perlen, Feingold, Silber geschwärzt
028 Brooch, 2009, polymethyl methacrylate, onyx beads, fine gold, blackened silver
98 x 76 x 40 mm
Privatsammlung/*Private collection*

029 Kette, 2009, Polymethylmethacrylat, Bergkristall-Perlen, Blattgold, Seide, Silber geschwärzt
029 Necklace, 2009, polymethyl methacrylate, rock crystal beads, gold leaf, silk, blackened silver
170 x 118 x 16 mm

030 Manschettenknöpfe, 2009, Vintage-Modeschmuck-Halbzeug, Silber geschwärzt
030 Cufflinks, 2009, vintage costume jewellery findings, blackened silver
h. ca. 30 mm

031

032

033

034

035

036

031 Objekt „LINGAM I", 2009, Polymethylmethacrylat, Vintage-Modeschmuck-Halbzeug,
Lack, Blattgold, Silber geschwärzt
031 Object "LINGAM I", 2009, polymethyl
methacrylate, vintage costume jewellery findings,
lacquer, gold leaf, blackened silver
h. 172 mm, dm. 52 mm

032 Manschettenknöpfe, 2009, Polymethylmethacrylat, Silber geschwärzt
032 Cufflinks, 2009, polymethyl methacrylate,
blackened silver
35 x 35 x 24 mm

033 Armreif, 2009, Acrylglas, Rauchquarz,
Blattgold, Silber geschwärzt
033 Bracelet, 2009, acrylic glass, smoky quartz,
gold leaf, blackened silver
145 x 136 x 65 mm

034 Manschettenknöpfe, 2009, Vintage-
Modeschmuck-Halbzeug, Silber geschwärzt
034 Cufflinks, 2009, vintage costume jewellery
findings, blackened silver
h. ca. 32 mm

035 Armreif, 2010, Polymethylmethacrylat,
Blatt-Weißgold, Silber geschwärzt
035 Bracelet, 2010, polymethyl methacrylate,
white gold leaf, blackened silver
124 x 120 x 60 mm

036 Ring, 2009, Vintage-Brosche,
Polymethylmethacrylat, Gold
036 Ring, 2009, vintage brooch,
polymethyl methacrylate, gold
38 x 40 x 27 mm
Privatsammlung/*Private collection*

037

038

041

039

040

042

037 Ausstellungsansicht „New Works",
Caroline van Hoek Contemporary Art Jewelry,
Brüssel 2009
*037 Exhibition view "New Works", Caroline van
Hoek Contemporary Art Jewelry, Brussels 2009*

038 Brosche, 2009, Polymethylmethacrylat,
Druckfarbe, Feingold, Blattgold, Silber
geschwärzt
*038 Brooch, 2009, polymethyl methacrylate,
printing ink, fine gold, gold leaf, blackened silver
115 x 100 x 25 mm*

039 Armreif „Libellen II", 2010, Polymethylmethacrylat, Perlen, zerstoßene Perlen,
Amethyst-Perlen, Blattgold, Silber geschwärzt
*039 Bracelet "Dragonflies II", 2010, polymethyl
methacrylate, pearls, crushed pearls, amethyst
beads, gold leaf, blackened silver
130 x 95 x 60 mm*

040 Armreif „Libellen I", 2009, Polymethylmethacrylat, Perlen, zerstoßene Perlen,
Amethyst-Perlen, Blattgold, Silber geschwärzt
*040 Bracelet "Dragonflies I", 2009, polymethyl
methacrylate, pearls, crushed pearls, amethyst
beads, gold leaf, blackened silver
120 x 85 x 100 mm*

041 Brosche, 2009, Polymethylmethacrylat,
zerstoßene Perlen, Strass, Amethyste, Feingold,
Blattgold, Silber geschwärzt
*041 Brooch, 2009, polymethyl methacrylate,
crushed pearls, rhinestones, amethysts, fine gold,
gold leaf, blackened silver
125 x 96 x 30 mm*
Collection de la Ville de Cagnes-sur-Mer,
Galerie Solidor

042 Ausstellungsansicht „New Works",
Caroline van Hoek Contempoaray Art Jewelry,
Brüssel 2009
*042 Exhibition view "New Works", Caroline van
Hoek Contemporary Art Jewelry, Brussels 2009*

043

044

046

047

048

045

045 Brosche, 2009, Polymethylmethacrylat, Strass, Druckfarbe, Lack, Blattgold, Silber geschwärzt
045 Brooch, 2009, polymethyl methacrylate, rhinestones, printing ink, lacquer, gold leaf, blackened silver
95 x 97 x 20 mm

046 Brosche, 2009, Polymethylmethacrylat, Amethyst, zerstoßene Perlen, Strass, Lack, Blattgold, Silber geschwärzt
046 Brooch, 2009, polymethyl methacrylate, amethyst, crushed pearls, rhinestones, lacquer, gold leaf, blackened silver
145 x 140 x 28 mm

047 Armreif, 2008, Polymethylmethacrylat, Vintage-Modeschmuck-Halbzeug, Strass, Kieselsteine, Lack, Blattgold
047 Bracelet, 2008, polymethyl methacrylate, vintage costume jewellery findings, rhinestones, pebbles, lacquer, gold leaf
115 x 115 x 54 mm

048 Brosche, 2009, Polymethylmethacrylat, Bergkristall-Perlen, zerstoßene Perlen, Strass, Lack, Blattgold, Silber geschwärzt
048 Brooch, 2009, polymethyl methacrylate, quartz crystal beads, crushed pearls, rhinestones, lacquer, gold leaf, blackened silver
120 x 68 x 25 mm

043–044 Ausstellungsansichten „New Works", Caroline van Hoek Contemporary Art Jewelry, Brüssel 2009
043–044 Exhibition views "New Works", Caroline van Hoek Contemporary Art Jewelry, Brussels 2009

049

050

051

053

052

054

049 Armreif, 2008, Vintage-Gürtelschnallen, Polymethylmethacrylat, Blatt-Weißgold
049 Bracelet, 2008, vintage belt buckles, polymethyl methacrylate, white gold leaf
88 x 105 x 56 mm

050 Ausstellungsansicht „OFF THE WALL II", Galerie V&V, Wien 2008
050 Exhibition view "OFF THE WALL II", Galerie V&V, Vienna 2008

051 Doppelring, 2009, Vintage-Gürtelschnalle (Cut-Steel-Imitation), Polymethylmethacrylat, Feingold
051 Double ring, 2009, vintage belt buckle (imitation cut steel), polymethyl methacrylate, fine gold
32 x 72 x 28 mm

052 Ring, 2008, Vintage-Brosche, Polymethylmethacrylat, Lack, Silber geschwärzt
052 Ring, 2008, vintage brooch, polymethyl methacrylate, lacquer, blackened silver
48 x 36 x 34 mm

053–054 Ausstellungsansichten „OFF THE WALL II", Galerie V&V, Wien 2008
053–054 Exhibition views "OFF THE WALL II", Galerie V&V, Vienna 2008

055

056

057

058

059

060

057 Kette, 2008, Polymethylmethacrylat, Amethyst-Perlen, Druckfarbe, Blattgold, Silber geschwärzt
057 Necklace, 2008, polymethyl methacrylate, amethyst beads, printing ink, gold leaf, blackened silver
Kunststoffelemente/*Plastic components:*
90 x 65 x 12 mm, 74 x 80 x 12 mm

058 Ring, 2008, Vintage-Brosche, Polymethylmethacrylat, Perle, Gold
058 Ring, 2008, vintage brooch, polymethyl methacrylate, pearl, gold
34 x 38 x 34 mm

059 Ring, 2008, Vintage-Brosche, Polymethylmethacrylat, zerstoßene Perlen, Silber geschwärzt
059 Ring, 2008, vintage brooch, polymethyl methacrylate, crushed pearls, blackened silver
42 x 57 x 42 mm
Privatsammlung/*Private collection*

060 Ring, 2008, Vintage-Brosche, Polymethylmethacrylat, Lack, Silber geschwärzt
060 Ring, 2008, vintage brooch, polymethyl methacrylate, lacquer, blackened silver
30 x 48 x 28 mm

055–056 Ausstellungsansichten „OFF THE WALL II", Galerie V&V, Wien 2008
055–056 Exhibition views "OFF THE WALL II", Galerie V&V, Vienna 2008

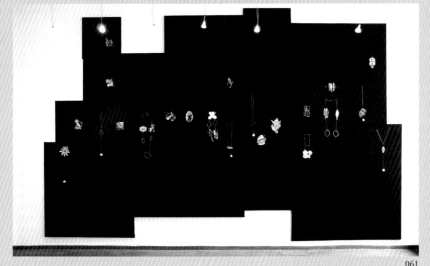

061

062

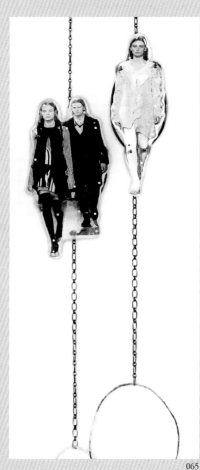

063

064

065

066

061 Ausstellungsansicht „OFF THE WALL II",
Galerie V&V, Wien 2008
Display: Wolfram Otto
061 Exhibition view "OFF THE WALL II",
Galerie V&V, Vienna 2008
Display: Wolfram Otto

062 Brosche, 2008, Polymethylmethacrylat,
Druckfarbe, Blattgold, Rosenquarz,
Rauchquarzperlen, Silber geschwärzt
062 Brooch, 2008, polymethyl methacrylate,
printing ink, gold leaf, rose quartz,
smoky quartz beads, blackened silver
178 x 135 x 36 mm

063 Ohrschmuck, 2007, Polymethylmethacrylat, Druckfarbe, Strass, Lack, Rauchquarz-
Perlen, Blattgold, Silber geschwärzt
063 Earring, 2007, polymethyl methacrylate,
printing ink, rhinestones, lacquer, smoky quartz
beads, gold leaf, blackened silver
74 x 82 x 35 mm

064 Brosche, 2007, Vintage-Gürtelschnallen,
Polymethylmethacrylat, Druckfarbe, Lack,
Blattgold, Silber geschwärzt
064 Brooch, 2007, vintage belt buckles, poly-
methyl methacrylate, printing ink, lacquer,
gold leaf, blackened silver
98 x 103 x 34 mm
Privatsammlung/ *Private collection*

065 Kette, 2008, Polymethylmethacrylat,
Onyx-Perlen, Lack, Blattgold, Gold,
Silber geschwärzt
065 Necklace, 2008, polymethyl methacrylate,
onyx beads, lacquer, gold leaf, gold,
blackened silver
Kunststoffelemente/ *Plastic components:*
125 x 70 x 19 mm, 127 x 48 x 19 mm

066 Brosche „Hexagonal Box", 2007,
Messing vergoldet, Rauchquarze, Lack,
Silber geschwärzt
066 Brooch "Hexagonal Box", 2007, gilded brass,
smoky quartz crystals, lacquer, blackened silver
87 x 104 x 40 mm

067

068

069

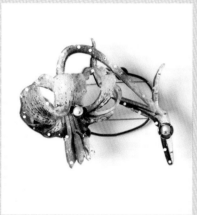

070

071

072

067 Kette mit Anhänger, 2006, Polymethylmethacrylat, Granate, Strass, Blattgold, Stahlseil
067 Necklace with pendant, 2006, polymethyl
methacrylate, garnets, rhinestones, gold leaf,
steel wire
Anhänger/*Pendant:* 97 x 67 x 8 mm
Privatsammlung/*Private collection*

068 Kette mit Anhänger, 2008, Polymethylmethacrylat, Vintage-Gürtelschnalle,
Druckfarbe, Amethyst-Perlen, Blattgold,
Silber geschwärzt
068 Necklace with pendant, 2008, polymethyl
methacrylate, vintage belt buckle, printing ink,
amethyst beads, gold leaf, blackened silver
Anhänger/*Pendant:* 112 x 92 x 37 mm

069 Brosche, 2008, Polymethylmethacrylat,
historischer Schwarzer Glasschmuck,
Druckfarbe, Onyx-Perlen, Blattsilber,
Silber geschwärzt
069 Brooch, 2008, polymethyl methacrylate,
historical black glass jewellery, printing ink,
onyx beads, silver leaf, blackened silver
88 x 94 x 26 mm

070 Brosche „Lili", 2008, Polymethylmethacrylat, Druckfarbe, Perlen, Tigerauge-
Perlen, Blattgold, Silber geschwärzt
070 Brooch "Lili", 2008, polymethyl
methacrylate, printing ink, pearls, tiger's eye
beads, gold leaf, blackened silver
90 x 108 x 20 mm

071 Brosche, 2007, Polymethylmethacrylat,
Druckfarbe, Lack, Blattgold, Silber geschwärzt
071 Brooch, 2007, polymethyl methacrylate,
printing ink, lacquer, gold leaf, blackened silver
130 x 125 x 14 mm

072 Objekt, 2007, Polymethylmethacrylat,
Druckfarbe, Lack, Blattgold, Messing
072 Object, 2007, polymethyl methacrylate,
printing ink, lacquer, gold leaf, brass
108 x 102 x 15 mm

073

074

075

076

077

078

073 Brosche „Ranunkel", 2007, Polymethylmethacrylat, Druckfarbe, Amethyst-Perlen,
Blattgold, Silber geschwärzt
*073 Brooch "Buttercup", 2007, polymethyl
methacrylate, printing ink, amethyst beads,
gold leaf, blackened silver*
95 x 140 x 8 mm
Privatsammlung/ *Private collection*

074 Ring, 2007, Vintage-Brosche,
Polymethylmethacrylat, Silber geschwärzt
*074 Ring, 2007, vintage brooch, polymethyl
methacrylate, blackened silver*
34 x 48 x 40 mm
Privatsammlung/ *Private collection*

075 Brosche „Amaryllis", 2008,
Polymethylmethacrylat, Druckfarbe,
Perlen, Blattsilber, Silber geschwärzt
*075 Brooch, "Amaryllis", 2008, polymethyl
methacrylate, printing ink, pearls, silver leaf,
blackened silver*
110 x 79 x 30 mm

076 Ausstellungsansicht „OFF THE WALL I",
Galerie OONA, Berlin 2007
*076 Exhibition view "OFF THE WALL I",
Galerie OONA, Berlin 2007*

077 Brosche „Colour Grid", 2007,
Polymethylmethacrylat, Druckfarbe,
Lack, Blattgold, Messing vergoldet
*077 Brooch "Colour Grid", 2007, polymethyl
methacrylate, printing ink, lacquer, gold leaf,
gilded brass*
62 x 93 x 25 mm

078 Ring, 2007, Polymethylmethacrylat,
Blattgold, Silber geschwärzt
*078 Ring, 2007, polymethyl methacrylate,
gold leaf, blackened silver*
48 x 45 x 38 mm

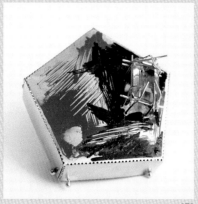

079

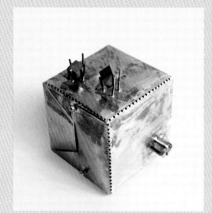

080

081

082

083

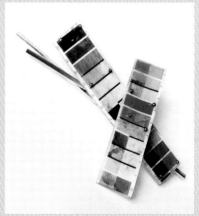

084

081 Brosche „Pyramide", 2007, Messing
vergoldet, Amethyst-Perlen
*081 Brooch "Pyramid", 2007, gilded brass,
amethyst beads*
63 x 64 x 56 mm
Privatsammlung/*Private collection*

082 Brosche, 2007, Polymethylmethacrylat,
Druckfarbe, Aquarellfarbe, Karneole, Onyx,
Messing vergoldet
*082 Brooch, 2007, polymethyl methacrylate,
printing ink, water colours, carnelians, onyx,
gilded brass*
89 x 89 x 25 mm

079 Brosche „Pentagon", 2007, Messing
vergoldet, Citrin, Lack, Gold
*079 Brooch "Pentagon", 2007, gilded brass,
yellow quartz, lacquer, gold*
63 x 66 x 35 mm

080 Objekt „Cube", 2006, Messing, Pyrite
080 Object "Cube", 2006, brass, pyrites
40 x 36 x 36 mm
Privatsammlung/*Private collection*

083 Brosche „X Colours", 2007, Polymethylmethacrylat, Druckfarbe, Blattgold, Messing
*083 Brooch „X Colours", 2007, polymethyl
methacrylate, printing ink, gold leaf, brass*
70 x 92 x 25 mm

084 Brosche „44 Colours", 2007,
Polymethylmethacrylat, Blattgold,
Messing vergoldet
*084 Brooch "44 Colours", 2007, polymethyl
methacrylate, gold leaf, gilded brass*
94 x 151 x 28 mm

085

086

087

089

088

090

085 Ausstellungsansicht „OFF THE WALL I",
Galerie OONA, Berlin 2007
Display: Wolfram Otto
085 Exhibition view "OFF THE WALL I",
Galerie OONA, Berlin 2007
Display: Wolfram Otto

086 Brosche „RGB", 2006, Polymethylmethacrylat, Granat-Perlen, Silber geschwärzt
086 Brooch "RGB", 2006, polymethyl
methacrylate, garnet beads, blackened silver
130 x 120 x 25 mm

087 Brosche „Box I", 2006, Messing vergoldet, Stahlseil, Silber geschwärzt
087 Brooch "Box I", 2006, gilded brass, steel
wire, blackened silver
35 x 44 x 13 mm

088 Brosche, 2007, Polymethylmethacrylat,
Rauchquarz-Perlen, Druckfarbe, Blattgold,
Messing vergoldet
088 Brooch, 2007, polymethyl methacrylate,
smoky quartz beads, printing ink, gold leaf,
gilded brass
102 x 89 x 32 mm
Privatsammlung/ *Private collection*

089–090 Ausstellungsansichten „OFF THE
WALL I", Galerie OONA, Berlin 2007
090 Exhibition views "OFF THE WALL I",
Galerie OONA, Berlin 2007

091

092

093

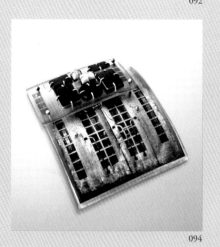

094

095

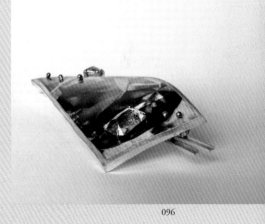

096

093 Armreif, 2007, Polymethylmethacrylat, Plastikarmreif, Vintage-Broschen und Halbzeug, Feingold
093 Bracelet, 2007, polymethyl methacrylate, plastic bracelet, vintage brooches and costume jewellery findings, fine gold
117 x 120 x 60 mm

094 Brosche, 2007, Polymethylmethacrylat, Onyx, Blatt-Weißgold, Silber
094 Brooch, 2007, polymethyl methacrylate, onyx, white gold leaf, silver
74 x 70 x 21 mm
Privatsammlung/*Private collection*

095 Brosche „Itten I", 2007, Polymethyl-methacrylat, Druckfarbe, Blattgold, Gold, Steinsynthese, Messing vergoldet
095 Brooch "Itten I", 2007, polymethyl methacrylate, printing ink, gold leaf, gold, synthetic gemstone, gilded brass
85 x 90 x 28 mm

096 Brosche, 2007, Polymethylmethacrylat, Druckfarbe, Strass, Blattgold, Messing vergoldet
096 Brooch, 2007, polymethyl methacrylate, printing ink, rhinestones, gold leaf, gilded brass
105 x 85 x 24 mm
Privatsammlung/*Private collection*

091–092 Ausstellungsansichten „OFF THE WALL I", Galerie OONA, Berlin 2007
091–092 Exhibition views "OFF THE WALL I", Galerie OONA, Berlin 2007

097

098

099

101

100

102

097 Brosche „Pamplona", 2003,
Polymethylmethacrylat, Strass, Blattgold, Silber
097 Brooch "Pamplona", 2003, polymethyl
methacrylate, rhinestones, gold leaf, silver
57 x 92 x 16 mm
Privatsammlung/*Private collection*

098 Brosche, 2004, Polymethylmethacrylat,
Glasperlen, Blattgold, Silber geschwärzt
098 Brooch, 2004, polymethyl methacrylate,
glass beads, gold leaf, blackened silver
122 x 78 x 14 mm
Privatsammlung/*Private collection*

099 Brosche „Diva V", 2004, Polymethylmethacrylat, Strass, Lack, Blattgold,
Silber geschwärzt
099 Brooch "Diva V", 2004, polymethyl
methacrylate, rhinestones, lacquer, gold leaf,
blackened silver
76 x 118 x 13 mm
Privatsammlung/*Private collection*

101 Ring „SVMMA TVLISSE IUVAT", 2002,
Polymethylmethacrylat, Pyrite, Perlen,
Blattgold, Silber vergoldet
101 Ring "SVMMA TVLISSE IUVAT", 2002,
polymethyl methacrylate, pyrites, pearls, gold leaf,
silver-gilt
29 x 68 x 44 mm

101–102 Ausstellungsansichten „Cut-Outs and
Pin-Ups II", Galerie V&V, Wien 2004
101–102 Exhibition views "Cut-Outs and
Pin-Ups II", Galerie V&V, Vienna 2004

103

104

105

106

107

108

103 Brosche „Pin-Up VIII", 2004, Polymethylmethacrylat, Strass, Blattgold, Silber
103 Brooch "Pin-Up VIII", 2004, polymethyl
methacrylate, rhinestones, gold leaf, silver
115 x 80 x 15 mm

104 Brosche „Bull Fight", 2004,
Polymethylmethacrylat, Strass, Blattgold,
Silber geschwärzt
104 Brooch "Bull Fight", 2004,
polymethyl methacrylate, rhinestones,
gold leaf, blackened silver
93 x 125 x 15 mm

105 Brosche „Sad Lady", 2003,
Polymethylmethacrylat, Strass, Blattgold,
Silber geschwärzt
105 Brooch "Sad Lady", 2003, polymethyl
methacrylate, rhinestones, gold leaf,
blackened silver
120 x 77 x 19 mm

106 Ring, 2002, Vintage-Gürtelschnalle,
Polymethylmethacrylat, Blatt-Weißgold, Gold
106 Ring, 2002, vintage belt buckle, polymethyl
methacrylate, white gold leaf, gold
34 x 45 x 43 mm
Privatsammlung/ *Private collection*

107 Brosche „Frühlingsreigen", 2003,
Polymethylmethacrylat, Strass, Blattgold, Silber
107 Brooch "Frühlingsreigen", 2003, polymethyl
methacrylate, rhinestones, gold leaf, silver
110 x 100 x 14 mm

108 Brosche „Diva X", 2004, Polymethylmethacrylat, Strass, zerstoßene Perlen,
Blattgold, Silber geschwärzt
108 Brooch "Diva X", 2004, polymethyl
methacrylate, rhinestones, crushed pearls,
gold leaf, blackened silver
102 x 84 x 17 mm
Privatsammlung/ *Private collection*

109

110

111

112

113

114

111 Brosche „Pin-Up I", 2003,
Polymethylmethacrylat, Strass, Pyrite,
Blattgold, Silber geschwärzt
111 Brooch "Pin-Up I", 2003, polymethyl
methacrylate, rhinestones, pyrites, gold leaf,
blackened silver
111 x 80 x 17 mm

113 Brosche „DA", 2004, Niello, Silber
teilweise geschwärzt
113 Brooch "DA", 2004, niello, partly
blackened silver
105 x 61 x 7 mm
Privatsammlung/*Private collection*

109–110 Ausstellungsansichten „Cut-Outs and
Pin-Ups III", Galerie OONA, Berlin 2004
109–110 Exhibition views "Cut-Outs and
Pin-Ups III", Galerie OONA, Berlin 2004

112 Ausstellungsansicht „Cut-Outs and
Pin-Ups III", Galerie OONA, Berlin 2004
112 Exhibition view "Cut-Outs and
Pin-Ups III", Galerie OONA, Berlin 2004

114 Ausstellungsansicht „Cut-Outs and
Pin-Ups III", Galerie OONA, Berlin 2004
114 Exhibition view "Cut-Outs and
Pin-Ups III", Galerie OONA, Berlin 2004

115

116

117

118

119

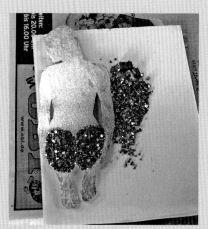

120

115 Brosche „Happy Heidi", 2003,
Polymethylmethacrylat, Strass, Pyrite,
Blattgold, Silber geschwärzt
115 Brooch "Happy Heidi", 2003, polymethyl
methacrylate, rhinestones, pyrites, gold leaf,
blackened silver
114 x 64 x 18 mm
Privatsammlung/ *Private collection*

116 Brosche „Golden Legs", 2003,
Polymethylmethacrylat, Granate, Strass,
Blattgold, Silber
116 Brooch "Golden Legs", 2003, polymethyl
methacrylate, garnets, rhinestones, gold leaf, silver
110 x 62 x 18 mm
Privatsammlung/ *Private collection*

117 Brosche, 2003, verschiedene Anhänger,
Niello, Silber
117 Brooch, 2003, various pendants, niello, silver
112 x 70 x 8 mm
Privatsammlung/ *Private collection*

118 Brosche „Kuss", 2003, Polymethylmethacrylat, Strass, Blattgold, Silber geschwärzt
118 Brooch "Kiss", 2003, polymethyl meth-
acrylate, rhinestones, gold leaf, blackened silver
70 x 71 x 14 mm
Privatsammlung/ *Private collection*

119 Ausstellungsansicht „Cut-Outs and
Pin-Ups III", Galerie OONA, Berlin 2004
119 Exhibition view "Cut-Outs and
Pin-Ups III", Galerie OONA, Berlin 2004

120 Brosche, 2003, Silber, Pyrite, Blattgold
120 Brooch, 2003, silver, pyrites, gold leaf
100 x 38 x 8 mm
Privatsammlung/ *Private collection*

121

122

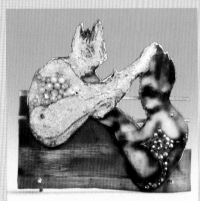

123

124

125

126

123 Brosche „Fußball I", 2003, Polymethylmethacrylat, Strass, Blattgold, Silber
123 Brooch "Soccer I", 2003, polymethyl meth-
acrylate, rhinestones, gold leaf, silver
102 x 122 x 16 mm

125 Halsschmuck, 2003, Polymethylmethacrylat, Blattgold, Gold
125 Necklace, 2003, polymethyl
methacrylate, gold leaf, gold
l. 580 mm
Privatsammlung/*Private collection*

124 Brosche „Synchronspringen", 2003,
Polymethylmethacrylat, Strass, Blattgold,
Messing
124 Brooch "Synchronized diving", 2003, poly-
methyl methacrylate, rhinestones, gold leaf, brass
75 x 77 x 10 mm
Privatsammlung/*Private collection*

126 Ausstellungsansicht „Glamourös",
Galerie OONA, Berlin 2001
126 Exhibition view "Glamourös",
Galerie OONA, Berlin 2001

121–122 Ausstellungsansichten „Glamourös",
Galerie OONA, Berlin 2001
121–122 Exhibition views "Glamourös",
Galerie OONA, Berlin 2001

127

128

129

130

131

132

127 Ring, 2000, Vintage-Brosche,
Polymethylmethacrylat, Gold
127 Ring, 2000, vintage brooch,
polymethyl methacrylate, gold
45 x 53 x 53 mm

128 Ausstellungsansicht „Glamourös",
Galerie OONA, Berlin 2001
128 Exhibition view "Glamourös",
Galerie OONA, Berlin 2001

129 Armreif, Ohrschmuck, 2000,
Polymethylmethacrylat, Blattsilber
129 Bracelet, earring, 2000,
polymethyl methacrylate, silver leaf
Armreif/ *Bracelet:* 84 x 74 x 49 mm
Ohrschmuck/ *Earring:* 75 x 52 x 12 mm

130 Ring, 2000, Vintage-Brosche,
Polymethylmethacrylat, Gold
130 Ring, 2000, vintage brooch,
polymethyl methacrylate, gold
45 x 56 x 33 mm
Privatsammlung/ *Private collection*

131 Ring, 2000, Vintage-Brosche,
Polymethylmethacrylat, Blattgold, Gold
131 Ring, 2000, vintage brooch, polymethyl
methacrylate, gold leaf, gold
45 x 51 x 32 mm
Privatsammlung/ *Private collection*

132 Ring, 2001, Vintage-Brosche,
Polymethylmethacrylat, Blatt-Weißgold, Gold
132 Ring, 2001, vintage brooch, polymethyl
methacrylate, white gold leaf, gold
47 x 53 x 52 mm
Privatsammlung/ *Private collection*

133

134

135

136

137

138

133 Armreif, 2000, Polymethylmethacrylat, Strass, Blattgold, Messing vergoldet
133 Bracelet, 2000, polymethyl methacrylate, rhinestones, gold leaf, gilded brass
93 x 93 x 75 mm

134 Ring, 2000, Vintage-Brosche, Polymethylmethacrylat, Blattgold, Gold
134 Ring, 2000, vintage brooch, polymethyl methacrylate, gold leaf, gold
44 x 62 x 40 mm
Privatsammlung/*Private collection*

135 Ring, 2000, Vintage-Brosche, Polymethylmethacrylat, Blattsilber, Gold
135 Ring, 2000, vintage brooch, polymethyl methacrylate, silver leaf, gold
42 x 45 x 42 mm
Privatsammlung/*Private collection*

136 Ring, 2000, Vintage-Brosche, Polymethylmethacrylat, Lack, Gold
136 Ring, 2000, vintage brooch, polymethyl methacrylate, lacquer, gold
42 x 46 x 36 mm

137 Fingerspange, 2000, Vintage-Brosche, Polymethylmethacrylat
137 Ring, 2000, vintage brooch, polymethyl methacrylate
44 x 68 x 20 mm
Privatsammlung/*Private collection*

138 Ring, 2000, Vintage-Brosche, Polymethylmethacrylat, Gold
138 Ring, 2000, vintage brooch, polymethyl methacrylate, gold
64 x 45 x 43 mm
Schmuckmuseum Pforzheim

139

140

141

142

143

144

139 Ring, 2000, Vintage-Brosche,
Polymethylmethacrylat, Gold
*139 Ring, 2000, vintage brooch,
polymethyl methacrylate, gold*
62 x 46 x 46 mm
Privatsammlung/*Private collection*

140 Ring, 2000, Vintage-Brosche,
Polymethylmethacrylat, Gold
*140 Ring, 2000, vintage brooch,
polymethyl methacrylate, gold*
46 x 38 x 32 mm
Privatsammlung/*Private collection*

141 Armreif, 2000, Polymethylmethacrylat,
Strass, Blattgold, Messing vergoldet
*141 Bracelet, 2000, polymethyl methacrylate,
rhinestones, gold leaf, gilded brass*
107 x 100 x 37 mm

142 Ring, 2002, Polymethylmethacrylat,
Rutilquarz, Silber
*142 Ring, 2002, polymethyl methacrylate,
rutile, silver*
36 x 26 x 30 mm

143 Ring, 2000, Ring, Polymethylmethacrylat, Gold
*143 Ring, 2000, ring, polymethyl
methacrylate, gold*
44 x 34 x 15 mm
Privatsammlung/*Private collection*

144 Ring, 2000, Vintage-Brosche,
Polymethylmethacrylat, Blattsilber, Gold
*144 Ring, 2000, vintage brooch,
polymethyl methacrylate, silver leaf, gold*
53 x 48 x 48 mm
Privatsammlung/*Private collection*

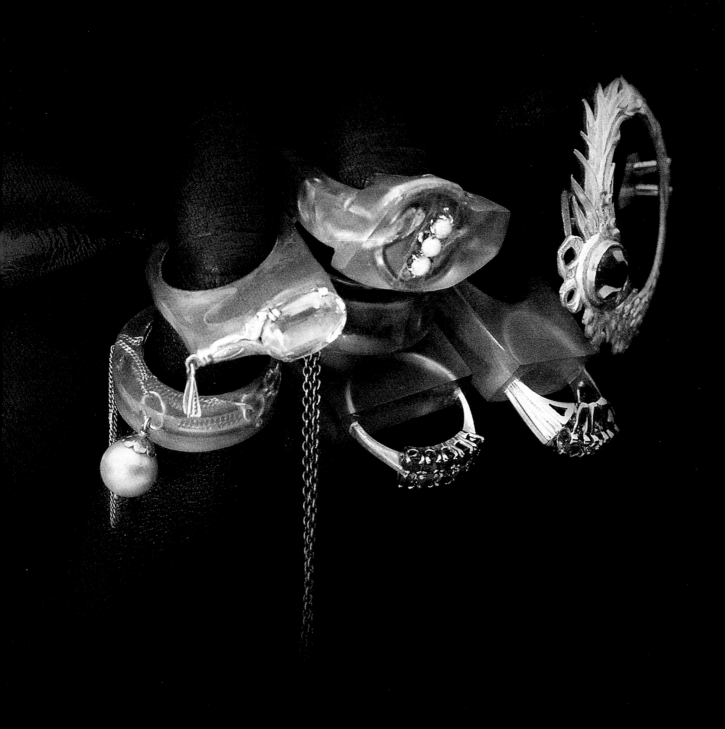

1975 in Graz geboren 1996–1998 Akademie für Kunst und Design Bratislava, Fachrichtung Schmuck und Metall bei Karol Weisslechner 1997–2002 Universität für angewandte Kunst Wien, Meisterklasse für Bildhauerei bei Brigitte Kowanz, Diplom 2002 | lebt und arbeitet in Wien

1975 born in Graz 1996–1998 Academy of Fine Arts and Design Bratislava, department of jewellery and metal, Karol Weisslechner 1997–2002 University of Applied Arts Vienna, Master class for Sculpture, Brigitte Kowanz, Diploma 2002 | lives and works in Vienna

Biographie | Biography

2012 MAK – Austrian Museum of Applied Arts/Contemporary Art, Vienna (AT) 2011 "Dodecade", Galerie OONA, Berlin (DE) 2010 "History Repeating II", Galerie Ornamentum, Hudson, NY (USA) | "History Repeating", Galerie Biró, Munich (DE) 2009 "New Works", Caroline van Hoek Contemporary Art Jewelry, Brussels (B) 2008 "Off The Wall II", Galerie V&V, Vienna (AT) 2007 "Off The Wall", Galerie OONA, Berlin (DE) 2004 "Cut-Outs and Pin-Ups III", Galerie OONA, Berlin (DE) | "Cut-Outs and Pin-Ups II", Galerie V&V, Vienna (AT) 2003 "Cut-Outs and Pin-Ups", Galerie Biró, Munich (DE) 2001 "Glamourös", Galerie OONA, Berlin (DE) 2000 "Schmuck im Schmuck", Galerie Biró, Munich (DE) | Galerie iBO, Klagenfurt (AT) 1999 "Vorher – Nachher", Galerie Tiller & Ernst, Vienna (AT)

Einzelausstellungen | Solo exhibitions

2010 "WUNDERWERK. Selected Works from Austria/Germany: 1970–2010", curated by Helen Drutt, Philadelphia Art Alliance, Philadelphia, PA (USA) | "Gegenwärtig – Schmuck in Österreich", 3. Eligius-Schmuck-Preis des Landes Salzburg 2010 (Preisträgerin/*Laureate*), Galerie im Traklhaus, Salzburg, MAK – Austrian Museum of Applied Arts/Contemporary Art, Vienna (AT) | "Lingam. Fertility Now", World Crafts Council BF, Mons (B), Museum Catharijneconvent, Utrecht (NL) | "GlassWear. Glass in Contemporary Jewelry", Mobile Museum of Art, Mobile, AL, Southeastern Center for Contemporary Art, Winston-Salem, NC (USA) 2009 "Lingam. Fertility Now", curated by Ruudt Peters, Konstfack, University College of Arts, Crafts and Design, Stockholm (S) | "Alice nel paese delle Meraviglie", Studio GR.20, Graziella Folchini Grassetto, Padua (I) | "GlassWear. Glass in Contemporary Jewelry", MAD – Museum of Arts and Design, New York, NY, Memorial Art Gallery of the University of Rochester, Rochester, NY, Art Museum of South Texas, Corpus Christi, TX (USA) | "Holiday Earring Show", Ornamentum Gallery, Hudson, NY (USA) 2008 "Gioielleria Contemporanea – Collezionismo a Padova", Studio GR.20, Graziella Folchini Grassetto, Padua (I) | "GlassWear. Glass in Contemporary Jewelry", Glazen Huis, Vlaams Centrum voor Hedendaagse Glaskunst, Lommel (B), Schmuckmuseum Pforzheim, Pforzheim (DE) 2007 "GlassWear. Glass in Contemporary Jewelry", curated by Ursula Neuman, Glass Pavilion, Toledo Museum of Art, Toledo, OH (USA) 2006 "2. Eligius-Schmuck-Preis des Landes Salzburg", Galerie im Traklhaus, Salzburg, Galerie V&V, Vienna (AT) |

Gruppenausstellungen (in Auswahl) | Group exhibitions (a selection)

"Holiday Earring Show", Ornamentum Gallery, Hudson, NY (USA) 2005 Galerie Gölles, Fürstenfeld (AT) (with Peter Skubic) | "Plastica. Oro Contemporanea", Studio GR.20, Graziella Folchini Grassetto, Padua, ENTRATALIBERA, Milan (I) | "Schwarzweiß", Galerie OONA, Berlin (DE) | "Schmucke Photographie", craft2eu, Hamburg (DE) | "Holiday Earring Show", Ornamentum Gallery, Hudson, NY (USA) | "Naturalismo, Memorialismo, Citazionismo nella Gïoelleria Contemporanea", Studio GR.20, Graziella Folchini Grassetto, Padua (I) 2004 "Fotografie – dreidimensional", Galerie V&V, Vienna (AT) | "GOLD", Galerie OONA, Berlin (DE) | "Divers Egal", Kleine Bronzen, University of Applied Arts Vienna (AT) | "modré z neba", Dizajn studio ULUV, Bratislava (SK) 2003 "ICE", a project of Sienna Gallery & Heller Gallery, New York, NY (USA) | "All That Glitters Isn't Gold", Sienna Gallery, Lenox, MA (USA) | "Re:View – Contemporary Jewellery from Austria", Wako, Tokyo (JP) | "10 Positionen zeitgenössischer Schmuckkunst", Werkstadt Graz, Graz (AT) | "ROSA", Galerie OONA, Berlin (DE) | "Travelling Symposium", Vitoria (ES) 2002 "wearables", Design Festival at the Central Academy of Fine Arts, Beijing (CN) | "SOS Museum", MAK – Austrian Museum of Applied Arts/Contemporary Art, Vienna (AT) | "der weibliche Blick", Haus der Kultur Infeld, Halbthurn (AT) | "Memorybank", Galerie Engelhorn, Vienna (AT) 2001 "Plateau Nord", contribution to the project "Bahnhof in Transition", Bahnhof Wien Nord, Vienna (AT) | "Schmuck lebt", Schmuckmuseum Pforzheim, Pforzheim (DE) | Galerie iBO, AVA-Hof, Salzburg (AT) 2000 "turning point", Künstlerhaus, Klagenfurt, Heiligenkreuzerhof, Vienna (AT) | "chrysler & greissler", a project of the

Engelhorn Galerien, Vienna (AT) | ”spektakulum”, Museum of Applied Art and Design, Tallinn (EE) | ”alles schmuck”, Inge Asenbaum Collection, museum of design zurich, Zurich (CH) | Symposium ”Gedachte Linie – Myslená čiara – Imaginary Line”, Samorín (SK) ”Kunst auf Zeit”, placard campaign in Graz (AT) | ”himmlisches jerusalem”, Kulturzentrum bei den Minoriten, Graz (AT) 1999 ”turning point“, NÖ Dokumentationszentrum für moderne Kunst, St. Pölten, (AT) | ”kontrakolaborace”, Kotelna, Prague (CZ) (with Peter Skubic) | Galleria Borghesi, Verona (I) 1998 ”auch-heinzundsusi“, Passagegalerie, Künstlerhaus, Vienna (AT) | ”Graz grüßt Villa de Bondt”, New Jewels Gallery, Gent (B) 1997 Galerie Spitzbart, Gmunden (AT) (with Peter Skubic) | ”sperk a dráhokam”, Internatioal Jewellery Symposium, Turnov (CZ)

Martina Windels "History Repeating II: Petra Zimmermann“, in: Metalsmith Magazine, Volume 31, no. 2/2011 | Susanne Längle ”3. Eligius Schmuckpreis des Landes Salzburg 2010. Gegenwärtig – Schmuck in Österreich“, in: Kunsthandwerk & Design, no. 6/2010, p. 01/12–9 | Susanne Längle (2010) ”Gegenwärtig – Schmuck in Österreich“, in: Parnass, no. 4/2010, p. 174–5 | Galerie im Traklhaus (ed.) (2010), 3. Eligius-Schmuck-Preis des Landes Salzburg 2010. Salzburg: Land Salzburg | Ruudt Peters, Guus van den Hout (eds.) (2010), Lingam. Fertility Now. Stuttgart: Arnoldsche Art Publishers | Andy Lim (ed.), Schmuckmuseum Pforzheim, CODA Museum Apeldoorn (co-eds.) (2009), The Compendium Finale of Contemporary Jewellers 2008. Cologne/New York: Darling Publications | Ursula Ilse-Neuman, Cornelie Holzach, Jutta-Annette Page (2007), GlassWear. Glass in Contemporary Jewelry. Stuttgart: Arnoldsche Art Publishers | Graziella Folchini Grassetto (2006), Plastica. Oro Contemporaneo. Padua: Studio GR.20 | Marthe Le Van (ed.) (2005), 500 Brooches. Inspiring Adornments for the Body. New York: Lark Books | Schnuppe von Gwinner (2005), “Schmucke Photographie“, in: Kunsthandwerk & Design, no. 3, p. 1, 4–11 | Antonia Kühnel (ed.) (2003), “Re-view, Aspekte Österreichischer Schmuckkunst“, Vienna | Graziella Folchini Grassetto (2003), “Casual and Chic“, in: Eyewear and Fashion, no. 19, p. 50–3 | New Resources. 2002 Design Festival, exhibition catalogue. Beijing: CAFA Beijing | Galerie Biró (ed.) (2002), Zeitgenössischer Kunststoff-Schmuck. Munich: Galerie Biró | Petra Zimmermann (2001), ”Zwischen Spannung und Balance“, in: Peter Skubic Between. Stuttgart: Arnoldsche Art Publishers, p. 103–5 | Lucia Oreská (2001), Gedachte Linie – Myslená čiara – Imaginary Line. Modra: ZOOM | Brigitte Felderer, museum für gestaltung zürich, et al. (eds.) (2000), Alles Schmuck. Baden: Müller | Charlotte Blauensteiner (2000), ”Kunst und Künstlichkeit“, in: Kunsthandwerk & Design, no. 3, p. 40–3 | Susanne Hammer, Fritz Maierhofer (eds.) (1999), Turning-point. Schmuck aus Österreich zur Jahrtausendwende. Vienna: Media-Plan | Illustrations for Alexandra Suess (ed.), Elmar Altvater (2000), Globalisierung – ein wissenschaftlicher Diskurs? Europäische Wissenschaftstage Steyr. Vienna: Passagen-Verlag | Eva Klingenstein (1999), ”Golden Girls“, in: Parnass, special edition, no. 15, p. 102–10

Autorenbiographien | Author Biographies

Barbara Maas

studierte Kunstgeschichte, Neuere Geschichte und Japanologie an der Ruhr-Universität Bochum, der Oxford University und der McMaster University/Kanada. Tätigkeit als Wissenschaftliche Mitarbeiterin, Kuratorin und Autorin. Seit 2003 Lehrbeauftragte für Kunstgeschichte und Theorie der Angewandten Kunst an der Fachhochschule Düsseldorf. Zahlreiche Buchpublikationen zur Architektur, Angewandten Kunst und Sozialgeschichte./ *Barbara Maas studied history of art, modern history and Japanese at Ruhr-Universität Bochum, Oxford University and McMaster University/Canada. She worked as research fellow, curator and author. Since* 2003 *she is lecturer in history of contemporary art and theory of applied arts at the University of Applied Sciences in Düsseldorf. She has published widely on architecture, applied arts and social history.*

Wolfram Otto

studierte 1995–1998 an der Staatlichen Akademie der Bildenden Künste in Karlsruhe Malerei und 1998–2002 an der Universität für Angewandte Kunst Wien Bildhauerei; lebt und arbeitet als freischaffender Künstler in Wien./ *Wolfram Otto studied Painting at the State Academy of Fine Arts Karlsruhe from* 1995–1998 *and Sculpture at the University of Applied Arts Vienna from* 1998–2002*; he lives and works as an independent artist in Vienna.*

Anna Schetelich

studierte Kulturwissenschaften und Kunstgeschichte an der Humboldt Universität Berlin. Tätigkeit als freie Mitarbeiterin an Museen u.a. am Deutschen Historischen Museum Berlin und Museum für Kommunikation Berlin. Seit 2000 Galeristin, Galerie OONA Berlin. Jurymitglied und Kuratorin bei internationalen Wettbewerben für zeitgenössischen Schmuck./ *Anna Schetelich studied cultural studies and history of art at the Humboldt University, Berlin. She worked as freelancer for different museums, such as the German Historical Museum and the Museum für Kommunikation Berlin. Since* 2000 *she is owner of OONA, Gallery for Contemporary Jewellery, Berlin. She is jury member and curator of international competitions in contemporary jewellery.*

Dank | Acknowledgements

an die Autoren/ *to the authors* Barbara Maas, Wolfram Otto und/*and* Anna Schetelich; an/*to* Dirk Allgaier und/*and* Marion Boschka von der ARNOLDSCHEN Verlagsanstalt/ *from ARNOLDSCHE Art Publishers;* an/ *to* Markus Böttcher, Katrina Daschner, Helfried Kodré, Merlin, Julie Monaco, Peter Skubic, Nurith Rittler, Vera Tollmann, Beatrix Vreča, Marie-Theres Zangger und an alle anderen, die zur Entstehung des Buches beigetragen haben/ *and to all who contributed to the development and creation of the book.*

© 2011 ARNOLDSCHE Art Publishers, Stuttgart, Petra Zimmermann, Wien/ *Vienna,* und die Autoren/ *and the authors;* Alle Rechte vorbehalten. Vervielfältigung und Wiedergabe auf jegliche Weise (grafisch, elektronisch und fotomechanisch sowie der Gebrauch von Systemen zur Datenrückgewinnung) – auch in Auszügen – nur mit schriftlicher Genehmigung der ARNOLDSCHEN Verlagsanstalt GmbH, Liststraße 9, 70180 Stuttgart./ *All rights reserved. No part of this work may be reproduced or used in any forms or by any means (graphic, electronic or mechanical, including photocopying or information storage and retrieval systems) without written permission from ARNOLDSCHE Art Publishers GmbH, Liststraße 9, D-70180 Stuttgart, Germany.*

Autoren | Authors Wolfram Otto, Wien/ *Vienna;* Dr. Barbara Maas, Mülheim an der Ruhr; Anna Schetelich, OONA, Gallery for Contemporary Jewellery, Berlin Übersetzung (Deutsch-Englisch) | Translation (German-English) Timothy M. Green, Brühl Grafik | Design Petra Zimmermann, Wien Offset-Reproduktionen | Offset-Reproductions Wolfram Otto, Wien, und/ *and* Repromayer, Reutlingen Druck | Printing Leibfarth & Schwarz, Dettingen/Erms

Bibliografische Information der Deutschen Bibliothek | Bibliographic information published by Die Deutsche Bibliothek Die Deutsche Bibliothek verzeichnet diese Publikation in der Deutschen Nationalbibliografie; detaillierte bibliografische Daten sind im Internet über http://dnb.d-nb.de abrufbar./ *Die Deutsche Bibliothek lists this publication in the Deutsche Nationalbibliografie; detailed bibliographic data is available on the Internet at http://dnb.d-nb.de.* **ISBN 978-3-89790-346-3**

Umschlag-Abbildung | Cover Illustration Doppelring, 2010 (Nr. 006)/ *Double ring, 2010 (no. 006)*

Bildnachweis | Photo Credits Alle Abbildungen/ *all photographs* © Petra Zimmermann außer/ *except of* S./ *p.* 21, 116, no. 113 Helfried Kodré, S./ *p.* 122/123 Chris Pfaff, S./ *p.* 125 Wolfram Otto

Ausstellungen | Exhibitions OONA, Gallery for Contemporary Jewellery, Berlin 12.02.–26.03.2011 | MAK, Österreichisches Museum für angewandte Kunst/ Gegenwartskunst, Wien (Frühjahr 2012)/ *MAK, Austrian Museum of Applied Arts/ Contemporary Art (spring 2012)*

Diese Publikation entstand mit finanzieller Unterstützung des Landes Steiermark/ *This book has been realised through the generous support of the Austrian state Styria*